I invite you to read this book with an open mind. If you think the evidence AGAINST Christianity is overwhelming, read on and discover that it is the evidence FOR Christianity that is overwhelming.

Kerby Anderson
National Director of Probe Ministries International, Host of *Point of View* Radio Show, Author, and Vice President of International Society of Christian Apologetics (2011)

Pat Zukeran understands the pluralistic, postmodern environment that is so frequently encountered today. If you are looking for answers to the same tough questions raised by skeptics as well as those in other religious traditions, check out this book. It gets right to the point in down to earth language that provides a firm foundation for those who want answers.

Gary R. Habermas
Distinguished Research Professor
Liberty University & Theological Seminary

It is with great enthusiasm that I recommend this much-needed and relevant book by Dr. Pat Zukeran. Brimming with powerful evidence and sound reasoning, Zukeran skillfully lays out the case for the truth of Christianity.

Dr. Ron Rhodes, ThD
President, Reasoning from the Scriptures Ministries
Adjunct Professor, Dallas Theological Seminary, Veritas Evangelical Seminary

Patrick Zukeran possesses a keen mind and a compassionate heart toward the peoples of the world who need a sensible presentation of the good news of the Lord Jesus Christ.

Ramesh Richard, PhD, ThD
President, RREACH International
Professor, Dallas Theological Seminary

Patrick Zukeran has made apologetics an inviting, practical, and personal presentation right from the introduction. His book is concise and easy to read. Yet there is enough substance to satisfy the academically oriented person who needs reliable supporting evidence.

Sam Tonomura
Executive Director Emeritus, Japanese Evangelical Missionary Society

I believe everyone should read this book. It will give the believers a strong basis on what they believe, and it is excellent for seekers who are trying to understand who they are, what they are doing here, and where they are going.

Fred Tow
Pastor, Houston Chinese Church

UNLESS I SEE ...
IS THERE ENOUGH
EVIDENCE TO BELIEVE?

PATRICK ZUKERAN

REDEMPTION
PRESS

Published by Redemption Press, PO Box 427, Enumclaw, WA 98022
Toll Free (844) 2REDEEM (273-3336)

Redemption Press is honored to present this title in partnership with the author.
The views expressed or implied in this work are those of the author. Redemption
Press provides our imprint seal representing design excellence, creative content
and high quality production.

Printed in the United States of America

This book is printed on acid-free paper.

Any people depicted in stock imagery provided by Thinkstock are models, and
such images are being used for illustrative purposes only.

Certain stock imagery © Thinkstock.

Because of the dynamic nature of the Internet, any web addresses or links
contained in
this book may have changed since publication and may no longer be valid.
Scripture quotations are from The Holy Bible, English Standard Version® (ESV®),
copyright © 2001 by Crossway, a publishing ministry of Good News Publishers.
Used by permission. All rights reserved.

ISBN 13: 978-1-63232-639-3 (Print)
        978-1-63232-636-2 (ePub)
        978-1-63232-638-6 (Mobi)

Library of Congress Catalog Card Number: 2011915539

This book is dedicated to the following men:

Dr. Norman Geisler: The man God used to strengthen my faith, motivate me to learn, and later in life, exhort me to persevere; a great defender of Truth; an inspiring teacher and gracious leader.

Dr. Robert Choun: The master teacher who taught me how to teach, how to inspire students and remains a model of grace in my life.

Dr. James Tan and Mike Foster: Men who have served the Lord faithfully in the Philippines demonstrating the power of God-given vision, never-ending passion, and always with the blessed touch of grace.

CONTENTS

FOREWARD
BY
NORMAN GEISLER, PHD

Never has there been a greater time than now for a book like this. Christianity is based on belief in a theistic God who created the world, who can do miracles, and who is the source of absolute truth and morality. All of these are rejected by our culture. So, we are proclaiming that the Word of God affirms Jesus is the Son of God who was raised from the dead by an act of God, and that this is the absolute truth about God to a world in which nearly half of its inhabitants do not believe in a theistic God. Yet there cannot be a Word of God if there is no God who can speak. Nor can there be acts of God if there is no God who can so act. Further, Jesus cannot be the Son of God if there is no God who can have a Son. What is more, Christianity certainly cannot be the absolute truth of God unless there is an absolute Mind who knows and reveals absolute truth.

In short, we cannot do evangelism in a non-theistic world without first doing pre-evangelism. They cannot start their evangelistic presentation with the Gospel when unbelievers in the culture do not even believe in the preconditions of the Gospel. Establishing the truth of these presuppositions is called apologetics. So, the need for apologetics has never been greater. This book helps fill this need. It covers the waterfront of these pre-evangelistic needs in a clear, concise, and comprehensive way. It has intellectual depth, but is written in a readable fashion.

Not only is there a need outside the church for apologetics books like this, the need has never been greater inside the church. Statistics show that some three quarters of our young people leave the church in their twenties and that the vast majority of them do not return. And a recent study revealed that the basic reason for their departure was doubts about the Bible.[1] These doubts begin in earnest in junior high school and are largely completed before they go to college. This bleeding must stop if the evangelical church is to survive. It cries out for the need to do apologetics within the church and among our young people.

Dr. Zukeran's book is particularly suited to help meet this need both inside and outside the church. Coming from a background in Buddhism and with a thorough training in apologetics, he has produced a credible, usable, and readable work that will help pastors, teachers, parents, and young people to understand and defend the faith in a faithless world. It not only is instructive on what we believe, but why we believe it. It effectively proclaims the changeless truth of the Christian faith in these changing times. Every young person and adult in the church needs this message.

Dr. Norman Geisler
Professor of Apologetics
www.VeritasSeminary.com

---

[1] Josh McDowell, *The Last Christian Generation* (Holiday, FL: Green Key Books, 2006), 13.

INTRODUCTION

A solitary figure sat alone in the restaurant gazing at the sea. As the morning sun glared off the water, he watched the fishermen scurry to and from their boats, some carrying fish, and others following with nets slung over their shoulders. There was a lot to think about. One associate had committed suicide, and the leader to whom he had entrusted his life and future lay rotting in a nearby grave. Was it all a mirage? Was it just an emotional experience that drew the heart of this young man away from his family and dreams to follow a new hope? What had he done, and how would he now put his life back together?

He took one last sip, placed his cup on the wooden table, paid for his meal, and departed the tiny inn. As he stepped out into the street, the sun rested directly above his head. It was noon. As his eyes adjusted to the sunlight, he heard three men calling his name. "Thomas! Thomas!" they shouted running toward him. With excitement in their voices and joy beaming out of their eyes, they bounded to him. "No, not them!" he thought. He did not want to have anything to do with these men ever again.

"We have seen the risen Lord!" they cried with childlike exuberance. Peter grabbed a firm hold of Thomas' left arm, placed his other hand on his shoulder, and looked directly into Thomas' eyes. "Thomas, it's true! He's alive! Jesus has risen from the dead just like He said He would. Indeed He is the Son of God! He is the Messiah whom we have been waiting for! He spoke with us, and I even touched him with these hands!" Peter held them up for Thomas to see. Peter's stare and tone of voice were very convincing, yet that was Peter. He was always the persuasive one. Thomas gazed into Peter's excited eyes and then turned. "No," he said taking a few steps away from the men. "As much as I would love to believe, I cannot. You men go on. I've got things to do."

I cannot get caught up in the emotion, Thomas thought to himself. *I will not devote my entire life and sacrifice my family and future again for something without convincing evidence.* Thomas slowly trudged down the street. His closest friend, John, shouted, "Thomas, wait!" Thomas turned around and saw his friend scurrying toward him. "Thomas, what will it take for you to believe?" John asked.

Thomas looked into the sincere, caring eyes of his best friend. He took a deep breath and then said, "Unless I see in his hands the mark of the nails, and place my finger into the mark of the nails, and place my hand into his side, I will never believe" (John 20:25). John knew his friend. Thomas was always the honest one. Of course it would be difficult for Thomas to believe in a man rising from the dead. John understood Thomas' response.

"Thomas, come with us. Hear the others. They have seen him too," John pleaded.

"All your talking and stories won't convince me, John. I need more! I am not going to just take your word for it. Show me the evidence!" Thomas replied angrily.

John put his right hand on Thomas' shoulder, and with the love of a concerned brother, he gently urged his friend, "Come with us one last time. I know how you feel, Thomas. I felt the same way when the women told me. When I saw his empty grave, I did not know what to make of it. But, Thomas, we have seen the risen Lord! Jesus is alive! He is the savior of the world! Come, just this final time, and listen to what we have to say."

It was not his words that coaxed Thomas into agreeing. It was the love and kindred spirit of his friend that made him reluctantly consent. "Alright," he said, "But this is the final time I will meet with you." Grudgingly, Thomas joined the other three and began walking with them to the house. *Could it be true?* Thomas thought to himself. *Could Jesus really be alive?* He paused, and then made this resolve in his heart: *Unless I see, I will not believe!*

Another Thomas

It was my first visit to a tiny church in Hawaii. Although I found the service nominally interesting, I was losing the battle to remain awake and began to drift into another world. I had been up till the late hours of the morning the previous night with friends reliving great moments in our sports careers and laughing over foolish antics we thought were so daring and bold. Now at the 10:00 a.m. service, I struggled to keep my eyes open. Finally losing the fight after the third hymn, I napped peacefully in the pew. Then something aroused me from my slumber. As I rubbed my eyes and gathered my senses, I realized the pastor was standing behind a table upon which rested bread and grape juice. This would be my first encounter with the Christian sacrament of "Communion."

The pastor explained this tradition to us. It was to commemorate the final supper Jesus had with his disciples before his sacrificial death on the cross that was to pay the price for the sins of the world. Then the pastor quoted two verses that changed my life forever. I can still hear the voice of that elderly man quote Matthew 11:28: "Come to me, all who labor and are heavy laden, and I will give you rest". I sat up in my chair, intrigued by what I had just heard. God wants to be a part of my life? The One who created the universe wants a personal relationship with me? In fact, He cares so much that He wants to carry the burdens of my life and give me rest?

As a high school student, I was dealing with adolescent insecurities, relational difficulties, poor grades, and an uncertain future. No one was interested in my struggles or the inner turmoil I was experiencing. Everyone had their own life to deal with, and no one had time to care about anyone else, much less a teenage boy many had already given up on. But the words of Matthew 11:28 caught my attention. I had been moving more toward atheism in my teen years. I felt even if there were a God, He certainly was not interested in the affairs of men, much less my insignificant life. I had never heard the Gospel message that He was deeply interested in my life, my deepest struggles, and that He wanted to give peace that I had never experienced in my tumultuous, adolescent years.

Then the pastor read the second verse. "Jesus said, 'And behold, I am with you always, to the end of the age' " (Matthew 28:20). My interest continued to grow. Not only was the God of the universe interested in me, He promised never to abandon me even in my worst moments. These words expressed a commitment greater than any I knew. The most significant promise we make in a lifetime is a marriage vow. Yet in a marriage vow, the final words are, "Till death do us part." God stated that not even death would separate us from Him. I was amazed that the God of the universe would desire to make such a commitment with one so undeserving like me. These two verses caught my attention, and I began to reflect on what I had heard.

The pastor gave the invitation, "If you would like to have a relationship with God and receive Christ as your Lord and Savior and have the assurance of eternal life with Him, repeat this prayer." The pastor led us in a prayer to receive Christ. I remember sitting in my pew and saying to God alone, "God, if this is real, if these promises are true, and you are the kind of God described in the Bible, I want to know you." It was then I trusted Christ and became a child of God.

I did not grow up in church, but I attended an Episcopalian school. I had learned some of the Bible stories, but never understood what Christianity was all about: a personal relationship with the God of the universe who has a deep interest in my life and has made a commitment to an eternal relationship. I reported this exciting news to my school priest that following Monday. With very little emotion, he acknowledged my story, and then told me not to take the Bible so seriously. He pointed out that there are many errors in the Bible, many of the stories are not accurate, and some are even fiction. His response was quite shocking to me. Suddenly, I began to question my newborn faith. Desiring to learn the Bible, I enrolled in my high school Bible class. The textbooks assumed that miracles were not possible, and instead, there were naturalistic explanations for the miracle accounts of the Bible. As I read the textbooks and listened to the class lectures, the Bible seemed to be filled with historical and chronological errors and stories borrowed from pagan mythology.

The evidence presented in these texts from history and archaeology appeared to be overwhelming. For example, Moses' crossing of the Red Sea really occurred at the Sea of Reeds. Some areas of this sea are only three feet deep. Any group of people could have easily made this crossing. Daniel was not written in sixth century BC as the book claims, but written much later in the second century BC because it contains Greek and Aramaic, languages unknown to a Jewish writer of Daniel's time. Therefore, the book is not historical in nature; it simply was given that appearance to encourage the Jewish people who were suffering under Roman persecution.

When it came to the New Testament, I discovered that the Gospels were written generations after the life of Christ. As time goes by, eyewitnesses depart from the scene, which allows for exaggerations and misinformation to creep into the accounts as they were passed on orally from one group to the next. Therefore, many of the accounts of Jesus were fiction or exaggerations that grew over the generations until the Gospels were finally written.

A natural conclusion that followed was that the resurrection was a legend. The disciples sincerely desired the words of Jesus to be true. The hope of the heavenly kingdom and the words of eternal life had to continue in order for the movement to grow. As His followers gathered, they felt His warm presence in a real way and went forth to preach a "risen" Jesus to a world that needed hope, even if their story was convoluted and contrived. Since many were in foreign lands, there was no way the converts could confirm or deny the message. Many took it by faith. It did not matter if Jesus' body was really in the grave; the disciples were sincere and their message of hope changed the world.

All that I was learning in Bible class was casting serious doubts on the credibility of the Christian faith. It seemed that Christianity was another nice religious story, but one with no historical basis. I searched for answers, but no one seemed to have any. My faith began to wane. Perhaps new faith was just another emotional experience? I refused to dedicate my life to a religion that said, "You just have to take a leap of faith." If Jesus did not rise from the dead, He was not the Son of God, and Christianity could not be true. Like Thomas, I needed to see the nail prints in Jesus' hands and feel His side. Was there good reason and evidence for faith in Christ? I said to myself, *Unless I see, I will not believe.*

After months of questioning, I sat at a restaurant with Ed, a friend from church. I shared with him all that I had learned in class, and that I had found no answers to these facts against Christianity. He looked at my discouraged countenance and said, "I do not have the answers, but this book may be able to help you." He gave me a book of Christian apologetics. I had never heard of the term *apologetics*. I came to learn it meant "a defense," and Christian apologetics was the defense of the Christian faith. I read it thoroughly. To my surprise, I discovered that Christianity was a rational and reasonable faith. There were indeed compelling reasons and evidence to support the foundations of the Christian faith. I found the material fascinating, and when I was finished, I proceeded to read another book and another. My quest for the truth had begun.

For those who are saying, "Unless I see, I cannot believe," I hope this journey will reveal the "nail prints in the hands" and the "pierced side" of Jesus, God's Son. I do not claim to have all the answers. In fact, there are times I wrestle with doubts. However, I believe there is enough evidence to make Christianity a more than reasonable choice.

CHAPTER 1

See the World through the Major Worldviews

At the foundation of all beliefs, world religions, and philosophies are worldviews. What is a worldview? A worldview is a set of presuppositions (assumptions which may be true partially true or entirely false), which we hold (consciously or subconsciously, consistently or inconsistently) about the basic makeup of our world.[1]

Every person holds to a worldview. Our worldview undergirds the way we interpret the world around us and guides us in the daily decisions that we make. It influences how we think about reality, morality, humanity, sexuality, epistemology (knowledge), cosmology, sociology, and theology. All areas of how we interpret the world and our experiences are filtered though our worldview. A person's worldview is intensely practical. Charles Colson states, "It is simply the sum total of our beliefs about the world, the 'big picture' that directs our daily decisions and actions."[2]

A worldview is like a pair of glasses we each wear, and through these glasses, we view and interpret the world around us. It is important that we are wearing the correct lenses; if you have ever put on a wrong pair of glasses, you know how distorted the world around you appears. If you continue to wear the wrong pair, it will be increasingly difficult

---

[1] James Sire, The *Universe Next Door* (Downers Grove: InterVarsity Press, 1988), 17.
[2] Sire, 18.

to maneuver around your environment. In the same way, it is critical that each person has the correct worldview. The wrong worldview will eventually lead to the wrong conclusions about reality and life.

It is for this reason that the search for truth begins with understanding worldviews. Interpreting the evidence from the wrong perspective will lead you to false conclusions. There are various worldviews, each one claiming to be true.

First Principles

There are some basic premises we must first begin with. These are called First Principles. First Principles are the foundation of knowledge. These are the premises with which we begin, for without them it is not possible to know anything. These are laws that do not need proofs because they are self-evident. Every person knows and applies these principles even if they do not know their formal titles.[3]

The First Principles begin with the premise that something exists. This universe exists, and we as conscious beings exist. Second is the Law of Noncontradiction, which states that contradictory claims cannot be true at the same time in the same way.[4] For example, the statements "God exists" and "God does not exist" cannot both be true at the same time and in the same way. If one of these statements is true, the other one must be false. The third is the Law of the Excluded Middle, which states that something either is or is not.[5] For example, either I am Pat Zukeran, or I am not Pat Zukeran. There is no other alternative. Finally, all worldviews require faith. This will be demonstrated in the sections to follow.

Some beliefs require a greater step of faith than others. For example, most people believe the universe has a beginning, and this first cause is called the "Big Bang." Can we be 100 percent certain that the universe began with the Big Bang? No, because none of us were there at this event. However, from the evidence, we can be reasonably sure or at least sure beyond a reasonable doubt. So the question we

---

[3]   Norman Geisler and Frank Turek, *I Don't Have Enough Faith to be an Atheist*, (Wheaton, IL.: Crossway Books, 2004), 62.

[4]   Ibid., 56.

[5]   Ibid., 62.

must ask ourselves is, "Is there good evidence to support my belief?" In other words, am I taking a step in the direction of the evidence?

These are the First Principles that guide us in discovering and discerning truth from error. These are the premises we accept, for they are self-evident truths and without them, it is not possible to know anything.

Identifying a Worldview

How do we identify another person's worldview? A person's worldview can be identified by the way he or she answers some fundamental questions. Philosopher James Sire lists seven basic questions every worldview must address, for they are the basic questions every human being must answer in their lifetime.[6]

The first question is, "What is the nature of God?" This is the primary question that most quickly distinguishes a worldview. Does a God exist? Is the material cosmos all that exists? If God does exist, how does one describe God? Are there many gods? Often, one's worldview is revealed in the answer to this question.

The second question is, "What is the nature of reality?" This is a question of metaphysics, which addresses the nature of the world around us. Is the external world an illusion? Is the world chaotic, or is it orderly and intelligently designed? Are God and the universe eternal and dependent on one another? Did God create the universe, and can He intervene in time and space? If God can intervene, are miracles possible?

The third question is, "How do you explain human nature?" This question addresses anthropology. In the movie *Contact*, actress Jodie Foster travels through a worm hole and meets an alien being who appears in the form of her deceased father. He states that his civilization has been studying the human race and finds that humans are a very curious species, capable of fulfilling both wonderful dreams and also horrific nightmares. How do we explain this paradox of human nature? Are we evolved animals? Are we gods in embryo form? Have we been created in the image of God but fallen in sin? The answer

---

[6] Ron Nash, *Worldviews in Conflict* (Grand Rapids: Zondervan Publishing, 1992), 55.

to this question plays a key role in the fields of psychology, sociology, and medicine.

The fourth question is, "How do you know that you know?" This question addresses epistemology, the study of knowledge and the question "How is knowledge attained?" Is it attained primarily through the senses? Is scientific knowledge the best method of attaining knowledge? Is it the only method? Can we know truth, or is truth relative? Much of modern philosophy concentrates on epistemology.

The fifth question is, "What happens to a person at death?" Is there life beyond the grave, or does a person cease to exist? Can we know if there is life beyond the grave? Although this is a question about death, our beliefs regarding death undoubtedly affect the way we live today.

The sixth question is, "How do you determine right and wrong?" This question addresses the area of ethics. Is there an absolute moral law code by which all people are to abide? Some believe that right and wrong are determined by the situation, and thus, right and wrong change depending on the situation in which one finds oneself. Others believe that right and wrong are relative and determined by the individual. A serious question arises when two cultures with different beliefs clash. How do we then determine right and wrong to resolve the conflict? A good example occurred on September 11, 2001 when radical Islamic terrorists hijacked two airline planes and used them to crash into the twin towers of the World Trade Center. The question arose as to how we determine a just response. America felt this was an act of war while the Taliban believed they were fulfilling Allah's will. Who is right in this situation? Our understanding of ethics is of crucial importance.

The seventh question is, "What is the meaning of history?" Is human history moving in a linear fashion toward some meaningful purpose? Some believe that human history has no ultimate purpose; it revolves in a never-ending circular cycle. If human history has a purpose, what is my role in this story? If human history has no ultimate purpose, we are forced to face the logical conclusion that our lives have no ultimate purpose.

These seven questions are the basic questions each worldview must answer. Every human being seeks answers to these basic questions in their lifetime. If one's worldview cannot answer any of these questions, it should be considered an incomplete worldview.

These questions are a great place to start when beginning a relationship with someone of a differing belief system. Too often, Christians want to preach their message; however, that can often alienate the individual, for no one enjoys being preached at. Instead, it is often more profitable to learn about another person's beliefs by asking questions about their worldview. In many of my discussions, some individuals simply accepted their beliefs and had never been challenged to examine and explain the reasons behind that which they believe. Through these questions, opportunities to point out inconsistencies or contradictions arise. Then opportunities to share reasons for faith in Christ will also arise. Instead of a combative debate, asking these questions, listening, and sharing reasons for your faith in Christ can lead to great discussions which cultivates the friendship.

Three Major Worldviews

There are three major worldviews that form the foundation upon which ideas, philosophical systems, and the world religions are built: theism, naturalism, and pantheism.

Theism

The basic tenet of theism is the belief in a personal God who created the universe out of nothing. Theistic religions include Christianity, Judaism, and Islam. Theism teaches that God created the universe but is not dependent on the universe. He is transcendent, but He is also immanent. In other words, He rules over the universe, but He is not totally distant. He is involved in sustaining the universe, is actively involved in history, and can be known by His creatures. He can intervene in time and space, thus miracles are possible.

Theism teaches that man is created in the image of God. This means that man possesses, in a limited finite way, some of the attributes of God, such as love, intelligence, emotion, and a will. However, despite being created in the image of God, man is a fallen and sinful being. This explains the paradox we find: man is indeed able to fulfill great dreams but is also able to carry out horrific nightmares.

Knowledge is attained through reason, experience, and divine revelation. Theists believe that there is life beyond the grave. Theists believe that man is composed of the physical body and also an immaterial soul that survives the death of the body. At death, every person will receive his or her judgment and eternal destiny. Morality is determined by our conscience, a moral law code imbedded in our hearts by God in whose image we are made and based upon God's law as revealed in His inspired revelation.

Theists believe that history is moving in a linear fashion. There is a purpose for our existence, and God is guiding the course of history to His ultimate goal.

Naturalism

The second worldview is naturalism. Naturalism teaches that the material universe is all that exists. Richard Dawkins writes, "An atheist in this sense of philosophical naturalist is somebody who believes there is nothing beyond the natural, physical world, no supernatural creative intelligence lurking behind the observable universe, no soul that outlasts the body and no miracles ..."[7]

Naturalists do not believe in the existence of a divine being or creator God. The universe is a cosmic accident, and there was no ultimate purpose for its conception. The universe operates according to the laws of nature; therefore, miracles are not possible. Naturalists teach several views of human nature. Most believe that man is an evolved animal. He is a material being, and there is no immaterial soul or consciousness that continues to exist beyond the death of the body.

For naturalists, knowledge comes through reason and experience. It is through our ability to reason, the five senses, science, and our experience that we attain knowledge. Since there is no God, there can be no divine revelation. There are several ways that the notion of right and wrong are determined within the framework of this view. Some naturalists believe that right and wrong are determined by the ones who are in power; in other words, might makes right. Another view is that right and wrong are determined by what produces the best

---

[7]   Richard Dawkins, *The God Delusion* (New York, New York: Houghton Mifflin Company, 2006), 35.

results for the greatest number, an ethic called utilitarianism. Others teach that right and wrong are determined by the situation. Each situation is different; therefore, right and wrong change according to the situation. Postmodern naturalists teach that there is no absolute right or wrong; they are instead relative and determined by each individual. Ultimately, naturalists will have a relative ethical system.

Naturalists believe there is no ultimate goal of history. One day the universe will die. As the universe continues to expand, it will lose energy, reach a state of final entropy, and come to an end. Like the universe, mankind will one day cease to exist. Therefore, in naturalism, history ultimately continues its aimless course, but ultimately all will end in extinction.

Pantheism

The third worldview is pantheism. *Pan* means all; *theism* means God. Pantheists believe God is an impersonal force made up of all things in the universe. In other words, God is the universe, and the universe is God. Pantheism is the foundation of many of the Eastern religions (i.e., Hinduism, many schools of Buddhism, Taoism), the New Age, and many animistic religions. Since God is one with the universe, the universe and God are eternal and dependent upon one another.

Since everything is a part of God, man is essentially divine. In Hinduism, there is a saying, "Atman is Brahman." Atman, or the immaterial essence of man, is identical with Brahman, the absolute, the impersonal force that pervades the universe.[8]

Knowledge is attained through enlightenment. Enlightenment is accomplished by attaining a "higher" level of consciousness, which is achieved in various ways. One of the most popular methods is through meditation, which, in many Eastern forms, involves emptying the mind and attaining a sense of unity with the divine, or the all-pervading force of the universe.

Pantheists adhere to the doctrine of reincarnation. After death, an individual will return in another form. Whether they return in a higher or lower form depends on the quality of the life they lived. This is

---

[8] Stephen Schumacher & Gert Woerner, ed., *The Encyclopedia of Eastern Philosophy and Religion,* (Boston: Shambhala Publications, 1994), 22.

the law of *karma*. The amount of good or bad karma one attains in this life determines the quality of life in the next reincarnation. It is hoped that one will continue to attain higher forms until the individual breaks out of the cycle of reincarnation and attains oneness with the divine. Just as a drop of rainwater journeys down the mountains, into the rivers, and then to the ocean, so the soul must find its way to union with the divine. Pantheists view history in a never-ending circular cycle that will continue to endlessly repeat itself.

These three worldviews are the foundation of the various philosophies and religions in the world today. Theism is the foundation for the world religions of Judaism, Christianity, and Islam. Naturalism is the foundation for the philosophies of Darwinism, Freudian psychology, Marxist Socialism, and even some of the world religions, such as some forms of Buddhism. Pantheism is the foundation of the Eastern religions, such as Hinduism, Taoism, and the New Age.

Tests of a Worldview

As one studies the major worldviews, it should become apparent that all three cannot be true at the same time for the reason that they hold contradictory positions. A basic law of logic is the *Law of Noncontradiction*, which states that opposites cannot be true at the same time and in the same sense.[9] This is a foundational premise of logic that is universally applied in all cultures. This law forms the foundation of rational thought.

It is a logical impossibility to believe, as the theist does, that God exists while simultaneously believing, as the naturalist does, that God does not exist, and conclude that both statements are true. If one is true, the other opposing view must be false. Likewise, it is also a logical impossibility to believe, as theists believe, the proposition that God is a personal being who created the universe and also adhere, as pantheists do, to the belief that God is a non-personal being who is interdependent with the universe. Again, both propositions cannot be true at the same time in the same way. How do we determine which

---

9   Norman Geisler, *Baker Encyclopedia of Apologetics* (Grand Rapids: Baker Books, 1999), 742.

worldview is true? There are indeed several ways to test a worldview to determine whether its tenets are true or in error.

Test of Correspondence

The first test is the *test of correspondence*. Truth is defined as that which corresponds with reality. There is a reality, and truth accurately describes and expresses it. Truth is telling it like it is. The propositions of a worldview or a religion should accurately describe and correspond with reality.

Pantheism teaches that the material world is an illusion. Does this correspond with reality? Darwinian Evolutionists, most of whom are naturalists, believe that living organisms all evolved from a single-celled organism. Does this conclusion correspond with the fossil evidence? Theists believe that an intelligent creator designed the universe. Does the evidence in nature reveal design? Propositions of a worldview should accurately describe the world and correspond with reality. Therefore, there should be evidence from the world around us that supports the tenets of a particular worldview.

Test of Consistency

The second test is the *test of consistency*. All the parts of a belief system should hold together in a logically consistent manner. Contradiction within a system is a sign of error.[10] For example, postmodern relativism is built on a naturalist worldview. Relativists teach that truth is relative; there are no absolute truths, only opinions of individuals or cultures. However, to say there are no absolute truths *is* an absolute truth. The relativist ends up acknowledging the premise he denies. This is a self-defeating statement because it is a contradiction.

Test of Comprehensiveness

The third test is the *test of comprehensiveness*. A worldview should be wide-ranging in scope and explain the world around us. It should explain much of the relevant data. What is discovered to be true in a variety of areas, such as history, our experiences, logic, the sciences, etc.,

---

[10]   Nash, 55.

should complement or support the worldview to which one adheres. If the data contradicts our worldview, we should reexamine our beliefs.

Pantheists teach that since the universe is divine, the universe is eternal. However, the scientific evidence does not support this tenet but rather goes against it. The scientific evidence indicates the universe has a definite beginning, which scientists refer to as the Big Bang. If the universe has a beginning, it cannot be eternal. This fact also presents a problem for the naturalist. The law of causality states that whatever has a beginning must have a cause. If the universe has a beginning, it must have a cause greater than it. Naturalists have yet to answer this dilemma. It goes against logic and science to say something came from nothing. The fields of science, especially astrophysics, physics, and cosmology do not support the premise of pantheism and naturalism. However, the data upholds the teachings of Christian theism, which states that "In the beginning, God created the heavens and the earth" (Genesis 1:1).

One's worldview or religion should explain the data from various areas. A worldview or religious system that cannot accommodate or chooses to ignore the facts from various areas should be reexamined.

The Test of Practice

The fourth test is the *test of practice*. Is a person able to consistently, albeit not perfectly, live out what he or she believes in the real world? For example, Buddhism teaches that suffering in this world is caused by desire. The goal of the Buddhist then is to eliminate all desire. Once desire is eliminated, one may attain enlightenment, and upon death, enter the state of Nirvana. However, is it possible to consistently live out a life absent of any desire? Isn't the aspiration to escape suffering a desire in and of itself?

The postmodern relativists teach that absolute truth does not exist. Since truth is relative, there are no moral absolutes. The individual determines right and wrong, and no one has the right to apply their standards on others. However, it is not possible to live out this premise consistently. If a relativist finds himself a victim of racial discrimination, he will quickly demand justice for this offense. However, this is not possible if there are no moral absolutes that apply to all people. In demanding fair treatment, the relativist is appealing to an absolute moral standard that applies to all individuals. One should be able to consistently live out the teachings of their belief system.

These four tests should be applied when examining a religion or philosophy. In pausing to reflect on these tests, you may realize you naturally use these four criteria when examining a belief system or teaching you encounter. For example, I remember listening to a pantheist on television teaching that once an individual attains oneness with the divine, they will not get sick or age. Immediately, I began to ask the questions, "Is this true to reality? Have I seen anyone defy sickness and aging? What about the laws of nature? Is this consistent with what we know in medical research? Does this teacher actually live out what he is teaching? Does he really expect to live eternally?" He must then not have a will or any plans of retiring or passing on his organization to his followers. We often, without realizing it, apply these tests in our daily life once we are aware of them.

I believe that Christianity is the only religion that passes these tests. The teachings of Christianity correspond to reality, and Christianity is comprehensive in its scope, is internally consistent, and can be lived out consistently. I believe that once you examine the evidence, you will see that Christianity is the only reasonable choice.

Our Starting Point

The purpose of apologetics is to transform lives for Christ by convincing minds and changing hearts. In order to persuade an individual to the truth of the Gospel, we need to begin at the right place, and that starting point is one's worldview. Before we can proceed to present a defense of the deity of Christ, we must first establish the premise that we live in a theistic universe.

If we do not establish the worldview of theism, the evidence we present will not be properly received. For example, if we present the case for the miracle of the resurrection without establishing the worldview of theism first, the naturalist will respond stating that miracles are not possible, and that there must be a naturalistic explanation for such miracle accounts that science will one day explain. A pantheist will respond by stating that Jesus is one of many avatars who have appeared, and that Jesus' miracles are typical of previous avatars.

However, if we establish the premise that God exists, and thus, we live in a theistic universe, the worldviews of naturalism and pantheism cannot be true. As a result, the religions and ideologies built on these worldviews will also ultimately be false. Also if God exists, there can be acts of God, and God can and does use miracles to confirm His message and His messengers. If God exists, there can be a Son of God and a Word of God, both of which should be affirmed by acts of God. Once we establish the premise that we live in a theistic universe, we establish the proper context to present our case for Christianity.

CHAPTER 2

See the Evidence for God

A World without God

I f God does not exist, man lives in a universe void of significance, purpose, and hope. If God is dead, then man is also dead. Atheist philosopher Friedrich Nietzsche illustrated this horrifying conclusion in his parable of "The Madman." In this story, the madman runs through the marketplace in hysteria screaming, "I am looking for God!" Mocked by the crowd, he soon realizes the vanity of his search and cries out in agony:

> Whither is God? I shall tell you. We have killed him—you and I. All of us are his murderers. But how have we done this? How were we able to drink up the sea? Who gave us the sponge to wipe away the entire horizon? What did we do when we unchained this earth from its sun? Whither is it moving now? Away from all suns? Are we not plunging continually? Backward, sideward, forward, in all directions? Is there any up or down left? Are we not straying as through an infinite nothing? Do we not feel the breath of empty space? Has it not become colder? Is not night and more night coming on all the time? Must no lanterns be lit in the morning? Do we not hear anything yet of the noise of the gravediggers who are burying God? Do we not smell anything yet of God's decomposition? Gods, too,

decompose. God is dead. And we have killed him. How shall we, the murderers of all murderers, comfort ourselves?[1]

Nietzsche realized and wrote in a stunning manner that, without God, man faces a hopeless future in a dark, cold universe while ever staring at his own extinction and one day the extinction of the universe itself. He realized that without God there can be no ultimate meaning for our existence and no basis for morality. The rejection of God leads to a dark and dreadful conclusion.

Void of Purpose without God

If there is no creator, the universe is a product of chance. In other words, it is an accident, and there was no intended purpose for our existence. Evolutionist George Gaylord Simpson states, "Man is the result of a purposeless and natural process that did not have him in mind."[2] In other words, if there was no intended purpose for our existence, there is no ultimate purpose or meaning for our existence. We began with no intended purpose, but our end is even more dreadful.

Scientists agree that the universe will continue to expand, reach a state of final entropy one day, and meet its end. The destiny of mankind is connected with the universe. As the universe will one day die, mankind will one day die and cease to exist. We live for a brief moment in this vast universe, and one day, we will become extinct never to exist again, never seeing our loved ones ever again. All our accomplishments, our joys, and dreams will one day end in annihilation. The only sure hope we have if God does not exist is death: our death, the death of mankind, and the death of the universe. We must then ask the question, "What difference does it make that we are ever here?" There was no intended reason for our existence, we live only for a short moment in time, and then mankind and the universe will cease to exist. What is it all for? We must ask ourselves,

---

[1] Friedrich Nietzsche, "The Gay Science," in The Portable Nietzsche, Walter Kaufman ed. (New York: Viking, 1954), 95.
[2] George Simpson, The Meaning of Evolution (New Haven, CT: Yale University Press, 1967), 344–45.

"What if the Big Bang never occurred? What difference would it have made?"

Atheists who have thought through the implications of their position have come to the conclusion that our lives are ultimately meaningless. Dr. William Provine, biology professor at Cornell University stated the implications of atheism clearly. He stated that God does not exist, there is "no life after death, no ultimate foundation for ethics and no ultimate meaning in life, no human free will."[3] Several years ago, I was listening to Nobel Prize-winning physicist Dr. Stephen Weinberg in a lecture at a debate at Baylor University on philosophical naturalism and intelligent design. In his opening statement, he said, "I am horrified at the thought that one day I will die and cease to exist, never to see my loved ones again. That thought horrifies me." Atheist philosopher Bertrand Russell wrote:

> Man is the product of causes which had no prevision of the end they were achieving; that his origin, his growth, his hopes and fears, his loves and his beliefs, are but the outcome of accidental collocations of atoms; that no fire, no heroism, no intensity of thought and feeling, can preserve an individual life beyond the grave; that all the labors of the ages, all the devotion, all the inspiration, all the noonday brightness of human genius, are destined to extinction in the vast death of the solar system, and that the whole temple of man's achievement must inevitably be buried beneath the debris of a universe in ruins ...[4]

Atheists who have thought through the implications of their naturalist worldview have all come to the conclusion that life without God is void of significance, purpose, and hope.

The legendary writer Ernest Hemingway portrayed this reality in several of his novels. I remember vividly the picture given to us in *The Old Man and the Sea*. In this story, Santiago, a seasoned fisherman, has fished for days in the gulf with no results. As a result, he loses the

---

[3]   William Provine quoted in Charles Colson, *How Now Shall We Live?* (Wheaton, IL.: Tyndale House Publishers, 1999), 92.

[4]   Bertrand Russell, *Why I Am Not a Christian* (New York: Simon & Schuster, 1957), 107.

respect of the villagers. Finally, he goes out farther than usual, and at noon, hooks a huge marlin. For three days, Santiago struggles with the huge fish until he finally captures it. However, the fish is too big for the boat, and he must tie the fifteen-hundred-pound beauty to the side of the boat.

Finally, he will receive respect as a master fisherman and earn a decent wage for his labor. But as he rows back to shore, sharks come and eat away at his fish. As the sharks attack, he courageously fights to keep his prize. However, there are too many attackers, and his strength runs out. By the time Santiago returns to shore, there is nothing left of his marlin but a skeleton. After his valiant struggle, Santiago has nothing to show.

As in life, each individual rows out to pursue the catch of a meaningful life through work, family, relationships, or whatever they choose as their fishing ground. One day, one seems to catch the big fish, the prize that will bring purpose: the dream job, the promotion, the girl of his dreams, the man of her dreams, financial security, and so on. However, as each person rides with their catch to shore, they realize that key prize will not survive the sharks of reality. Slowly, they eat away at their worth. As Santiago fought to protect his fish, so each person fights to protect his or her dream. But in the end, there are too many sharks, and eventually they win. As the old man returned to the docks with nothing, each person, after all the efforts of their life, ends up with nothing but a skeleton. One day, we will eventually die, and all that we had worked for will be forgotten and left in ruins. The work of a medical researcher who discovers cures for diseases, the politician who fights for justice, the scientist who makes wonderful discoveries, their works are all ultimately meaningless, for in the end it all will lie in ruins with the death of mankind and the universe. Each individual realizes in the end that we must live out our existence in a meaningless and hopeless universe doomed for extinction. In the end, Hemingway shot himself, a victim of the atheist existential philosophy.

Centuries before modern philosophers, Solomon explained this truth in the book of Ecclesiastes. After turning away from God and indulging in a life of pleasure, he concluded, "Vanity of vanities, says the Preacher, vanity of vanities! All is vanity. What does man gain by all the toil at which he toils under the sun? A generation goes, and a generation comes, but the earth remains forever ... There is no remembrance of former things, nor will there be any remembrance of later things yet to be among those who come after" (Ecclesiastes 1:2–11). Solomon's words sound much like the writings of modern atheist existentialist writers.

Morality is Meaningless without God

If God does not exist, morality becomes meaningless as well. What difference does it make if I live like Mother Theresa or Adolf Hitler? If there is no lawgiver, there is no universal moral law. Furthermore, as Provine stated, there is no foundation for ethics. If there is no universal moral law, right and wrong become relative. Eventually, right and wrong will be determined by the one who is in power, a might-makes-right kind of ethics. This has led to disastrous consequences. Instead of a utopia, atheist philosophy has led to one of the bloodiest centuries in human history. Adolf Hitler murdered over six million Jews. Joseph Stalin murdered nearly double the amount of Hitler. Mao Tse Tung, the man who said religion was the opium of the masses, murdered over thirty million. All these men, heavily influenced by naturalist philosophy, did not create a utopia but a horrific nightmare. If there is no universal moral law to appeal to, how can we say what occurred at Auschwitz was wrong?

Atheism has not led to a utopia but instead has left mankind empty and bewildered. One of the tests of a worldview is if it can be lived out consistently. On this test, atheism fails miserably. No atheist can consistently live out the implications of their worldview. Atheists attempt to live for a purpose and often appeal to a universal moral law. Bertrand Russell, despite being an atheist, fought for social justice and was a critic of war and sexual restrictions.

I was speaking at a church, and after the service, an atheist named Derrick wanted to meet with me for coffee to challenge my points. I listened to his justification for atheism and then asked him, "Derrick, if God does not exist, what is the meaning of your existence? Why do you wake up in the morning?"

"The purpose for our lives is to propagate the human species," he answered with great confidence.

I then asked him, "Why is that a good and meaningful purpose? Mankind is doomed to extinction along with the death of the universe. If our existence is an accident, why does it really matter if we pass our genes on to another generation when we are doomed to annihilation?"

He paused and thought for a while. No one had ever pushed him to consider the ultimate end of his worldview. He then stated, "It is important for people to face reality and the truth. That we are here with no ultimate purpose of life after death."

I then asked him, "Why should anyone care about that? If we live a meaningless existence, why are you so passionate about telling everyone our lives have no ultimate meaning?"

Derrick paused for a moment and was rescued by his atheist companion, who quickly tried to change the subject.

Next time you dialogue with your atheist friend, ask him, "If God does not exist, what is the meaning of life?" Push him down the road, and he will soon discover the implications of his worldview. This is not positive evidence for the existence of God, but it points out the implication that atheism is irrational and unlivable. When your atheist friend discovers the unreasonableness of his position, this often softens a hardened heart to receive another perspective.

If God exists, significance, purpose, and hope are found in a relationship with the One who created all things. Christianity is a rational and livable belief system. Is there evidence that supports a belief in God? Fortunately, I believe there is enough evidence to support a belief in God. The evidence makes theism a more reasonable choice than atheism.

Mission Impossible

Can anyone be absolutely certain that God does not exist? An honest individual must admit it is impossible to be absolutely certain of this. The reason is that one must know all there is to know about the universe in order to say with certainty that God does not exist anywhere in the universe.

Allow me to illustrate this point. Suppose I said, "I am absolutely certain that there are no nails in my house." To be completely sure of this fact, I would have to search every corner and inch of my house. When I have complete knowledge of every area of my house, it is then and only then that could I say, "I am certain there are no nails in my house." Likewise, to say, "I am absolutely certain that God does not exist," means I have to know all there is to know of the universe. Only when I have full knowledge of the universe can I be certain that God does not exist anywhere in the universe.

However, how much does man know about the universe? A fair-minded individual would have to admit that we know less than 1 percent of all that there is to know. Since it is not possible for us to attain full knowledge of the universe, no individual can conclusively prove that God does not exist somewhere in the universe. A fair-minded individual must entertain the possibility that a God exists. It is thus impossible to conclusively prove the atheist position. In other words, the atheist position requires a step of faith. As stated in the previous chapter, all worldviews require faith, and atheism is no exception. The key is to put your faith in what is true. An intelligent person will step in the direction from which the evidence is pointing; in fact, the evidence points to an intelligent creator.

Similar to the previous section, this is not positive evidence for the existence of God but rather it points out the impossibility of atheism's certainty. Often, atheists do not realize that their position also requires faith. Hopefully, this realization will open up a hardened heart to consider the possibility that God exists.

Something from Nothing?

Why does the universe exist, and what explains its origin? The cosmos present compelling evidence for the existence of God. The first question we must answer is, "Does the universe have a beginning, or is it eternal?" There is compelling scientific and philosophical evidence that the universe is not eternal, but that it has a beginning.

Scientific Evidence for a Beginning

The overwhelming majority of scientists now affirm that the universe has a beginning, and that it came into existence with a cataclysmic explosion called the Big Bang. Agnostic astronomer Robert Jastrow presents several scientific discoveries that build a conclusive argument for the Big Bang. I will present only five of these arguments, which can easily be remembered because they each begin with the letter "R": relativity, red shift, radiation afterglow, ratio of key elements, and a running-down universe.

First, Einstein's theory of general *relativity* predicted an expanding universe. In the early twentieth century, scientists assumed that the universe was eternal. Physicists attempted to develop a theory that would demonstrate how the universe could remain stable without collapsing in on itself due to the force of gravity. In 1917, Einstein introduced his theory of general relativity, which attempted to show the universe could remain in a steady state. However, Einstein made one of his greatest mistakes, known as the "fudge factor": At one point in his equation, he divided by zero. A Russian mathematician, Alexander Friedman, pointed out this error, and Einstein reluctantly admitted his mistake. Einstein was greatly troubled by the results of his equations because it indicated that the universe is expanding; thus, the universe exploded into being. He reluctantly admitted the universe is not eternal but has a beginning.[5]

The discovery of the *red shift* confirmed Einstein's theory. Scientists Milton Humason and Edwin Hubble discovered that the galaxies are moving away from the earth and one another at an extraordinary speed of nearly one hundred million miles an hour. Astronomers discovered that as a galaxy moves away from the earth, its redness increases. The degree of color transition allows scientists to measure the speed at which the galaxies are traveling. The red shift revealed that the universe continues to expand. This movement of galaxies away from one another is the result of an original cataclysmic explosion that set the galaxies in such a motion. As a result of this discovery, scientists can calculate what would occur if we move backward in time: We would return

---

[5] Robert Jastrow, *God and the Astronomers* (New York: W. W. Norton & Company, 1992), 17-21.

to a time when the universe was condensed into a dense mass. It is from this point that the universe exploded into existence.[6]

A third form of evidence was the discovery of the *radiation afterglow* from the original explosion. Two physicists named Ralph Apher and Robert Herman proposed a theory that if the universe had exploded into existence, there would have been an intense radiation following the explosion resembling the fireball that follows the explosion of a hydrogen bomb. Thus, there should be an afterglow of this radiation from this original fireball spread consistently throughout the universe. In 1965, physicists Arno Penzias and Robert Wilson were measuring radiation in the sky when they discovered that the earth was encompassed by a glow of radiation coming from every direction. Using a large horn antenna, they picked up microwave signals and low-level background noise coming from whatever direction they pointed their new detector. The radiation could not be coming from the sun only but rather from the entire universe. This afterglow is what one would expect from the Big Bang explosion. The scientists had discovered the radiation from the original fireball explosion of the universe. This was one of the most significant discoveries in science, and Penzias and Wilson won a Noble Prize for their discovery.[7]

Robert Jastrow expresses the significance of this finding as follows: "The clincher, which has convinced all but a few doubting Thomases, is that the radiation discovered by Penzias and Wilson shows a characteristic pattern of intensities at different wavelengths and frequencies of radiation that matches the pattern of the radiation produced in an explosion."[8]

Fourth is the *ratio of key elements*: hydrogen, helium, and deuterium. The universe today is made up of 73 percent hydrogen, 24 percent helium, and 3 percent heavier elements.[9] This ratio is what would be expected if the universe were the result of an explosion. After the Big Bang explosion, neutrons and protons would have joined transforming hydrogen into helium. This process would have lasted approximately

---

[6]   Ibid., 11-13.
[7]   Ibid., 67-70
[8]   Ibid., 70.
[9]   Hugh Ross, *Creator and the Cosmos* (Colorado Springs, CO.: NavPress, 1995), 20.

thirty minutes, and after that period, the cooling temperature and decreasing density would have halted the creation of helium. Scientist predicted then that approximately 25 percent of the matter in the universe would have been transformed to helium. Advanced instruments today allow us to measure amounts of helium in distant stars; that amount is nearly 25 percent in the universe, thus affirming the Big Bang prediction of scientists.[10] Deuterium is found consistently throughout the universe. This element is formed in extremely high temperatures generated by a large explosion. The fact the Deuterium is found throughout the universe indicates a large explosion had taken place. One large explosion would explain the consistency of this material throughout the universe.[11]

Fifth is that the universe is *running down*. This is important because of the first and second laws of thermodynamics. Norman Geisler summarizes the relevance of this law in reference to the beginning of the universe:

The second law of thermodynamics is the law of entropy. It asserts that the amount of *usable* energy in any closed system is decreasing. This must be held in tension with the first law of thermodynamics, the law of the conservation of energy, which states that the amount of *actual* energy existing within the universe changes form, yet remains constant. As energy changes to less usable forms of energy, the closed system of the universe is running down; everything tends toward disorder. ...Now if the overall amount of energy stays the same, but the universe is running out of usable energy, then the universe began with a finite supply of energy. This would mean that the universe could not have existed forever in the past. If the universe is getting more and more disordered, it cannot be eternal. Otherwise, it would be totally disordered by now, which it is not. So it must have had a highly ordered beginning.[12]

---

10   Jastrow, 80–81.
11   Francis Collins, *The Language of God,* (New York: Free Press, 2006), 45.
12   Norman Geisler, *Baker Encyclopedia of Christian Apologetics.* (Grand Rapids, MI.: Baker Books, 1999), 102.

Jastrow states, "The universe is running down like a clock. If it is running down, there must have been a time when it was fully wound up."[13] In other words, the universe is running out of usable energy. Therefore, if we go backward in time, there was a moment when the energy was at its maximum state of availability. Jastrow further states, "The universe was wound up like a clock at this moment, and everything that happened since has been its unwinding."[14]

Here is a simple illustration. A few times, I have left the lights of my car on overnight. When I arrive in the morning, I realize my lights are dimmer than the day before, my car has less energy, and I cannot start my engine. The fact that my car battery is losing energy shows that there was a time in the past when it had maximum energy. If my car lights were on for a few weeks, it would have no energy left. In the same way, if the universe was eternal and infinitely old, all the energy would have been used up. The fact that the universe has usable energy shows it has a beginning when there was maximum energy available.

Returning to the car illustration, from the moment I drive my car out of the car dealership, it is running down. Eventually, it will break down and be unusable. We can usually tell the age and usage of a car by the state of decay it is in. In the same way, the universe is running down, and things in the universe go from order to disorder. If the universe were infinitely old, it would be in a state of disorder.

These scientific discoveries have convinced the majority of scientists that the universe has a beginning. Nobel Prize-winning physicist and atheist Stephen Weinberg describes the original explosion in his book, *The First Three Minutes* as not "an explosion like those familiar on Earth, starting from a definite center and spreading out to engulf more and more of the circumambient air, but an explosion which occurred simultaneously everywhere, filling all space from the beginning with every particle of matter rushing apart from every other particle."[15]

---

13   Jastrow, 32-33.
14   Ibid., 113.
15   Stephen Weinberg, *The First Three Minutes* (New York: Basic Books, 1985), 5, quoted in Lee Strobel, *The Case for a Creator* (Grand Rapids, MI.: Zondervan Publications, 2004), 94.

Philosophical Evidence for a Beginning

There is good scientific evidence for the Big Bang, but there is also philosophical support that points to a beginning or a first cause that is eternal. The fact that today, this present moment, is the end of history shows there must have been a beginning in the finite past. The reason is that it is not possible to traverse an infinite past. Today would not have arrived if there had been an infinite number of days prior to today, for there would be no starting point to bring us to this moment.

Allow me to illustrate this. It is possible to count from zero to fourteen billion (estimated age of the universe). It would take a while, but it can be done because we have a starting point. However, it would not be possible to count to fourteen billion beginning from negative infinity. The reason is that you would never have a starting point because you would go back infinitely. Thus, philosophically, the universe must have a beginning because it is not possible to traverse an infinite past. There must be a starting point, and whatever has a beginning must have a cause. This leads to one of the most powerful arguments for the existence of God.

The First Cause

The fact that the universe has a beginning presents a strong case for God because of the law of causality. The law of causality states that whatever has a beginning must have a cause. This is the basis of the cosmological argument which utilizes the law of causality.

The cosmological argument goes like this: [16]

1. Whatever has a beginning must have a cause.
2. The universe has a beginning.
3. Therefore, the universe must have a cause.

From this point, we must identify the cause of the universe. It is unreasonable to conclude that the universe came into existence from nothing. Nothing does not exist, and therefore, cannot be a causal

---

[16]   Geisler, *Baker Encyclopedia of Christian Apologetics,* 399.

agent of anything. This goes against logic and all that we know in science and our experience.

The most reasonable conclusion is that the universe is the result of a cause that is greater than it. Material effects must have an adequate cause, and the effect cannot be greater than its cause. Therefore, whatever created the universe is greater than the universe. A creator or God is a reasonable first cause.

Some ask, "Where did God come from?" This question derives from a misunderstanding of the cosmological argument. The law of causality states that whatever begins to exist must have a cause. God does not have a beginning; He is eternal. The Bible states, He is from "Everlasting to everlasting" (Psalm 90:2). Remember, it is not possible to traverse an infinite past. There must be a starting point, an eternal first cause, which existed before the universe. Einstein's theory of relativity states that time, space, and matter are all codependent on one another. Before the universe, there was no time, no matter, and no space. Therefore, whatever created the universe is eternal, for time did not exist until the Big Bang. An infinite cause must have created the finite universe, and an eternal existing cause must have created time.

The evidence supports the premise that the universe does indeed have a beginning. Scientifically, this has been supported by Einstein's theory of relativity, the red shift, radiation afterglow from the Big Bang, the ratio of key elements, and the running down of the universe. The beginning of the universe is also supported philosophically because one cannot traverse an infinite past. There must have been a beginning, and whatever has a beginning, must have a cause, a first mover, an eternal causal agent that set the universe and time in motion. This is the most reasonable conclusion.

Not only does the cosmological argument present a great challenge for the atheist, it also poses a huge problem for the pantheist. In pantheism, God and the universe are one. They are mutually dependent on one another; one cannot exist without the other. Therefore, the universe is believed to be eternal. However, if the universe has a beginning, it cannot be eternal. Thus, the cosmological argument refutes the worldviews of naturalism and pantheism. In fact, the discoveries of the original explosion begin to point ever increasingly to the Genesis account.

Agnostic astronomer Robert Jastrow concludes saying, "Now we see how the astronomical evidence leads to a biblical view of the origin of the world. All the details differ, but the essential element in the astronomical and biblical accounts of Genesis is the same, the chain of events leading to man commenced suddenly and sharply, at a definite moment in time, in a flash of light and energy."[17]

The Cosmic Machine

The second argument for the existence of God is the argument of design, or the teleological argument. The argument is the following:

1. Every design has a designer.
2. The universe has highly complex design.
3. Therefore, the universe has a designer.[18]

This was illustrated by William Paley, who gave the famous watch illustration. Utilizing his illustration, I present it with a little twist from the islands. If you were walking along the beach of a deserted island and discovered a watch, what would you immediately assume? Would you assume the natural forces like the waves, wind, lightning, and sun formed the watch over a long period of time, or would you assume someone else is on the island and dropped their watch? No one in his right mind would assume, "Wow, what a great feat of evolution! I am amazed at how Mother Nature created this watch over millions of years." We know that natural forces cannot create something so orderly and complex. We could even disassemble the watch and leave it on the beach for millions of years, but it would never become a watch again. In order to create a watch, an intelligent being must come and assemble the parts into a watch. Specified order and complexity point to a designer.

---

[17] Jastrow, 14.

[18] Norman Geisler and Frank Turek, *I Don't Have Enough Faith to be an Atheist* (Wheaton, IL.: Crossway Books, 2004), 95.

Complexity and design are found in every facet of the cosmos. In fact, the more we are learning in the sciences, the more we are discovering precise engineering of many complex parts for a specified purpose. The odds of our universe arising from random accidental acts grow more and more unlikely with the discoveries we continue to make.

Let's begin with the forces of the universe. Scientists today have observed that we live in a universe that appears to have been made for human life. Innumerable factors have somehow fallen into precise order to allow human life on planet earth. Scientists call this the *anthropic principle*. Scientist Patrick Glynn states, "The anthropic principle says that all the seemingly arbitrary and unrelated constants in physics have one strange thing in common—these are precisely the values you need if you want to have a universe capable of producing life."[19] So not only did the universe have a beginning, it appears to have been precisely engineered for human life. We live in a "just right" universe.

There are four fundamental forces of physics in the universe: gravity, strong nuclear, weak nuclear, and electromagnetism. These forces affect nearly everything in the universe. Adjusting these forces just slightly would be disastrous. Glynn lists a few examples of what would happen if these forces were just slightly altered:[20]

1. Gravity is roughly 10^{39} times weaker than electromagnetism. If gravity had been 10^{33} times weaker than electromagnetism, stars would be a billion times less massive and would burn a million times faster.

2. The nuclear force is 10^{28} times the strength of gravity. Had the weak force been slightly weaker, all the hydrogen in the universe would have been turned to helium (making water impossible, for example).

3. A stronger nuclear force (by as little as 2 percent) would have prevented the formation of protons—yielding a universe without atoms. Decreasing it by 5 percent would have given us a universe without stars.

---

[19]   Patrick Glynn, *God the Evidence* (Rocklin, CA.: Prima Publishing, 1997), 22.
[20]   Ibid., 29.

4. If the difference in mass between a proton and neutron were not exactly as it is—roughly twice the mass of a electron—then all neutrons would have become protons or vice versa.

Hugh Ross notes that the universe expands at just the right rate. If the universe expanded faster, matter would disperse, and the formation of galaxies and stars would not be possible. If its expansion were slower, matter would cluster and eventually the universe would collapse on itself. Ross further adds, "This expansion rate cannot differ by more than one part in 10^{55} from the actual rate."[21] These are just a few examples of just how precise these forces are balanced in the universe to make life possible.

Ross lists more examples of factors that fell into place just in our galaxy and solar system that made life possible on the earth:[22]

1. The earth is just the right distance from the sun. Adjust it just 2 percent and life on earth would not be possible. Two percent farther and water would freeze, but 2 percent closer and water would evaporate too quickly.

2. Jupiter is just the right size and positioned in just the right place so that it acts as a large vacuum protecting the earth from comets and asteroids that would otherwise strike the earth.

3. Our planet rotates at just the right speed. A few percentages slower and the temperature changes between night and day would be too great. If it rotated quicker, wind velocities would be too great and have destructive effects.

4. The earth tilts at just the right angle. If the tilt were greater or less, the surface temperatures would be too great.

5. The moon is just the right size, so its gravitational pull stabilizes our axis tilt and creates wave activity so that sea waters are cleansed and replenished.

---

21 Ross, 116.
22 Ibid., 139–141.

6. We have just the right oxygen quantity in the atmosphere. If it were greater, plants and hydrocarbons would burn up. If it were less, animals would have too little to live on.

7. The earth is just the right size with the right surface gravity. If it were greater, the planet's atmosphere would retain too much ammonia and methane. If it were weaker, the planet's atmosphere would lose too much water.

8. The earth has just the right plate tectonic activity. If the activity were any greater, too many life forms would be destroyed. If there were less activity, nutrients on the oceans floors would not be recycled.

9. The earth's crust is just the right thickness. If it were any thicker, too much oxygen would be transferred from the atmosphere to the crust. Any thinner and the volcanic and tectonic activity would be too great.

10. The earth has just the right carbon dioxide level in the atmosphere. If it were greater, we would have a runaway greenhouse effect. If it were less, plants would be unable to maintain efficient photosynthesis.

Hugh Ross goes on to list nearly one hundred factors that went right in our universe and solar system that makes life on earth possible; this list does not exhaust all the factors that are necessary. For instance, water is a necessary ingredient for life, and it just so happens that it has very unique properties. When water freezes into a solid state, it becomes lighter than its liquid form, and therefore, it floats. If this did not occur, life at the bottom of the ocean would freeze and die, and the earth would be covered in ice.[23] An innumerable amount of factors came together to make life on earth possible.

Design is also evident in living organisms. For example, the human brain is a highly complex machine. We have yet to create a computer that can do all that the human brain is capable of. Agnostic astronomer, Carl Sagan, stated that "the genetic information in the human brain expressed in bits is probably comparable to the total number of

---

[23]   Glynn, 22.

connections among neurons—about one hundred trillion, 10^{14} bits. If written out in English, say, that information would fill some twenty million volumes, as many as are stored in the world's largest libraries ... The brain is a very big place in a very small space ..."[23] He went on to note that "the neurochemistry of the brain is astonishingly busy, the circuitry of a machine more wonderful than any devised by humans."[24] If we would not assume the watch evolved by chance, how much more would that hold true of the human brain, which is undoubtedly more complex?

The human body is a well-designed machine made up of hundreds of complex systems working in perfectly complementary fashion. With each movement of my hands, hundreds of neurons and electrical impulses are going back and forth from my brain, down my spine, and to my fingers at thousandths of seconds in perfectly timed sequences. Scientist and engineers spend hours in research and corporations pay millions to create robots that can mimic only some of the capabilities of the human body. If we saw a mechanical robot moving across a parking lot, we would not assume it came together as a result of natural forces. Why would we then assume that natural forces somehow formed the human body?

One of the most compelling examples of design is DNA. DNA is a long, helical structure that looks like a twisted ladder located in the nucleus of a cell. It is composed of four nitrogen bases adenine, guanine, cytosine, and thymine represented by the letters A, G, C, and T. This four-letter molecule-alphabet is arranged in very precise order, the combinations of which determine the genetic makeup of living organisms. These four bases are arranged in differing but exact combinations forming different amino acids, which are the building blocks of proteins; these then form the molecules in cells.

Scientists often use our alphabet as an analogy to bring deeper understanding of DNA combinations. Our alphabet has twenty-six letters. These letters are arranged into different sequences and combinations to form words to communicate. These letters must be in the

---

[23] Carl Sagan quoted in Norman Geisler, *Baker Encyclopedia of Christian Apologetics.* (Grand Rapids, MI.: Baker Books, 1999), 278.
[24] Ibid., 278.

right order and combination to make any sense. In the same way, DNA provides information which comes from an intelligent source. If you were walking on the beach and saw, "John loves Mary" in the sand, you would not assume this was the result of natural forces. You would immediately assume that an intelligent being was the source because the presence of such information assumes an intelligent source.

What makes DNA a powerful evidence of design is that an incredible amount of information is contained in a single cell. Twelve hundred to two thousand letters or bases are needed to build one protein. It is highly improbable that a single protein molecule could form by chance. Stephen Meyer states that the probability of the right amino acids forming the precise sequence needed to form one protein molecule is one chance in a hundred thousand trillion trillion trillion trillion trillion trillion trillion trillion trillion trillion trillion. That is a ten with 125 zeros behind it.[25] He further states that this would be the odds for just one protein molecule. "A minimally complex cell needs between three and five hundred protein molecules."[26] Francis Collins, the scientist who led the Human Genome Project describes the complexity of the DNA information in the human body.

> The human genome consists of all the DNA of our species, the hereditary code of life. This newly revealed text was three billion letters long and written in a strange, cryptographic four—letter code. Such is the amazing complexity of the information carried within each cell of the human body, that a live reading of the code at a rate of one letter per second would take thirty-one years, even if reading continued day and night. Printing these letters out in regular font size on normal bond paper and binding them all together would result in a tower the height of the Washington Monument.[27]

In comparing DNA to a computer program, Microsoft's Bill Gates stated that DNA is far, far more complex than any software

---

[25]   Steven Meyer quoted in Lee Strobel, *The Case for a Creator* (Grand Rapids, MI.: Zondervan Publishing, 2004), 225.
[26]   Ibid.,, 229.
[27]   Francis Collins, *The Language of God*, (New York: Free Press, 2006), 1-2.

ever created.[28] We would not assume the Microsoft Windows program was the result of a monkey banging on a computer keyboard. In fact, my friends in computer programming spend hours studying programs looking for the one-digit error that keeps a program from working properly. One digit out of sequence can ruin a program. The sequencing in the DNA code is even more complex and precise in its sequencing.

As scientists continue to unravel the mysteries of the universe, they find themselves face-to-face with the realization of the apparent design and order of the universe. British astrophysicist Dr. Fred Hoyle states, "A superintellect has monkeyed with physics, as well as chemistry and biology."[29] The more we discover in those and other fields of science, the more we realize the near impossibility of life evolving by mere chance. Physicist Dr. Robert Griffiths, who won the Heinemann prize in mathematical physics, states, "If we need an atheist to debate, I go to the philosophy department. The physics department isn't much use."[30]

Order and design of the universe points us to the haunting probability of a designer. Astronomer Dr. George Greenstein writes, "As we survey the evidence, the thought insistently arises that some supernatural agency—or rather, Agency—must be involved. Is it possible that suddenly, without intending to, we have stumbled upon scientific proof of the existence of a Supreme Being?"[31]

The quest of science appears to lead us back to Genesis 1:1: "In the beginning, God created the heavens and the earth." NASA scientist and self-proclaimed agnostic Dr. Robert Jastrow sums up the circular journey of science. "For the scientist who has lived by faith in the power of reason, the story ends like a bad dream. He has scaled the mountains of ignorance; he is about to conquer the highest peak; as he pulls himself over the final rock, he is greeted by a band of theologians who have been sitting there for centuries."[32]

---

28 Bill Gates, quoted in Lee Strobel, *The Case for a Creator*, 225.
29 Fred Hoyle, quoted in Hugh Ross, *The Creator and the Cosmos* (Colorado Springs: NavPress, 1995), 121.
30 Robert Griffiths quoted in Ross, 124.
31 George Greenstein, quoted in Ross, 121.
32 Jastrow, 102.

When an atheist is asked the critical questions of, "How do you explain the apparent order and design in the universe?" and "How did it come to be?" the most common answer I am given is, "It just happened. As immense as the odds are, it just happened." To believe that the universe in all of its complexity and order "just happened" requires a leap of faith. Another even more critical question to ponder is which position requires greater faith: the theist who believes that the cause of the universe is a divine creator or the atheist who proposes that a random mass explosion created the universe by accident? The latter requires more faith. In fact, I often tell my atheist friends that I admire them for their great faith. From the study of the great universe through the telescope to the study of the universe under the microscope, in all areas we discover evidence of an intelligent designer.

What Does Your Conscience Tell You?

A third line of evidence for God is the Moral Argument:

1. Everyone adheres to a universal moral law.
2. A universal moral law implies a moral lawgiver.
3. Therefore, there must be a supreme moral lawgiver.

Everyone has an innate sense of right and wrong. Proof of a universal moral law is demonstrated when examining the ethical codes of societies and religions of the world. All cultures value human life. In all cultures, adultery, murder, rape, and stealing are wrong and punishable acts. We did not have to learn this; we simply know that stealing and killing innocent people are wrong. Even the worst criminals in jail can suffer a sense of guilt for their crime. In fact, we consider those who commit heinous crimes with no sense of guilt functionally insane.

These ethical standards may be expressed in different ways, but cultures around the world express similar standards of right and wrong. For example, all people agree a man may not take any women he wants to for his possession. All cultures value the covenant of marriage. It is true that some cultures may allow a man to marry more than one wife; however, he must enter into the covenant of marriage. Within the marriage covenant, adultery is wrong. Even in polygamous cultures, a husband and his wives are expected to remain faithful to one another.

I was once asked in a seminar to address the following statement: "There are cultures that do not value human life. Cultures that practice cannibalism show they do not value human life." In fact, cannibalistic cultures show a high regard for human life. In these cultures, cannibalism is practiced for two reasons. The first reason is that it is the greatest form of revenge on an enemy. Cannibalism is the greatest type of revenge because the human body and life is so special that to desecrate it is to inflict the greatest pain on one's enemy. The second context in which it is performed is when a great warrior or leader dies. The followers will eat his body believing his spirit will abide in them. Here cannibalism is practiced as the greatest honor. Individuals so value the deceased leader that they want his memory and presence to remain with them. The practice of cannibalism is immoral, but my point here is that cultures which practice cannibalism understand the value of human life. C.S. Lewis wrote:

> Some people say the idea of a Law of Nature or decent behavior known to all men is unsound, because different civilizations and different ages have had quite different moralities. But this is not true. There have been differences, but these have never amounted to anything like a total difference. If anyone will take the trouble to compare the moral teaching of, say, the ancient Egyptians, Babylonians, Hindus, Chinese, Greeks and Romans, what will really strike him will be how very like they are to each other and to our own.[33]

This moral law code is evident in all cultures and is present within us from a very young age. Even little children will argue over issues defending their sense of justice. We often hear them saying, "That's not fair!" Where do we acquire this sense of right and wrong? A universal moral law points to a moral lawgiver.

The thought of hydrogen atoms evolving into thinking beings with a conscience, will, and ability to reason is inconsistent with scientific

---

[33] C.S. Lewis, *Mere Christianity*, (New York, NY: Macmillan Publishing, 1960), 19.

observation and sound reasoning. A purposeful and moral being cannot arise from impersonal, lifeless matter. Naturalists assert that we are simply material beings, beings made of matter. However, morality is not tied to matter. Morality is nonmaterial like love, justice, and beauty are nonmaterial. Therefore, morality comes from an immaterial and personal source.

A moral law code must come from a moral lawgiver whose character is reflected in His moral law code. It is His image we now reflect. Romans 2:14–15 states that our creator instilled within us a conscience that is universal to all men. Being created in the image of God means we reflect the moral qualities of our creator.

A universal moral law code is not only evident in all people, it is undeniable. Moral relativists who deny a universal moral law suddenly acknowledge one when they experience unjust treatment. For example, they may say racism is fine if that is what some cultures want to believe. However, when they are a victim of unjust discrimination, they will quickly scream for justice, pointing to a universal moral law by which they expect their perpetrators to abide.

I remember speaking to a man from China who was espousing moral relativism. I asked him, "Would you consider Hitler's actions against the Jews right and just?" He responded without hesitation, "Yes! If that is what Hitler thought was right, then it was right. Morality is determined by the individual and culture. There is no universal moral law!" Then I asked the next question knowing he was from China. "Is what the Japanese did in Manchuria in World War Two right and just?" He suddenly looked upward and sideways; I could see he was beginning to rethink his position because now he was being hit on a personal level. He paused, and then hesitatingly said, "Well, I guess it was right if that is what the Japanese felt was right." I then asked, "Then why does the Chinese government continue to demand that Japan apologize for what occurred there? They should just drop the whole issue and declare no crime occurred." Now my friend was clearly struggling. If he said Japan should apologize, he would be appealing to a universal moral law that holds all men and nations accountable. If he says Japan should not apologize, he was going against his moral conscience.

Whenever a suspect with overwhelming evidence of his guilt gets off free from a trial, people respond with outrage over the sense of injustice they just witnessed. For example, in 1995, O.J. Simpson was proclaimed innocent of the charge of murdering his ex-wife Nicole and Ronald Goldman despite what was believed to be overwhelming evidence. After his release, men and women came out to protest, and hundreds held signs outside the courthouse and Simpson's house for months. The human soul cannot rest until justice is served. This sense of justice is powerful in each individual.

A universal moral law is undeniable and is evident in all cultures. We could not live in society without it. Moral relativism is not livable; it fails the test of practice. Society would quickly degrade into anarchy if all individuals did what was right in their own eyes. On September 11, 2001, terrorists hijacked two airline jets and flew them into the World Trade Towers in New York. What was the response of the nation? Everyone knew the terrorist organization responsible had to be brought to justice. By doing so, everyone was acknowledging a universal moral law. For the next few weeks, I waited to hear the relativists boldly proclaiming their philosophy, but I found none. There was no one shouting, "These terrorists are simply living out their beliefs. They are simply products of their culture, and we should allow them to express their faith and form of justice as they were taught. We should tolerate their beliefs as equally valid and true as ours." The voices of the relativists were absent. Everyone was seeking a just response, but justice on whose terms? There could be no justice unless there was a universal moral law code we knew all people must acknowledge and by which they must abide.

Atheists argue that God does not exist because of the presence of evil. However, acknowledging the presence of objective evil indicates there is a universal standard of good from which we have deviated. C.S. Lewis struggled with this as an atheist. He wrote, "My argument against God was that the universe seemed so cruel and unjust. But how had I got this idea of just and unjust? A man does not call a line crooked unless he has some idea of a straight line. What was I comparing this universe with when I called it unjust?"[34] Thus, even the

---

[34]   C.S. Lewis, *Mere Christianity*, 45.

argument of evil rather than disproving God becomes further evidence of a universal moral standard of good derived from a moral lawgiver.

One of the most popular objections is that the sense of morality is simply the result of the Darwinian evolutionary process. Our sense of morality is our instinct for self-preservation and propagation of the human race. Atheists believe we are simply material beings; however, as I mentioned earlier, morality is not tied to matter. Our sense of morality is beyond the material. Our sense of morality is different from our instinct of self-preservation. Suppose you see a boy drowning in a pool of deep water but realize you are not a strong swimmer. You will feel two desires: one to jump in and help at the risk of your life, and another to keep yourself out of danger and preserve your life. You soon will struggle between these two instincts, for there is something that tells you that you must help rather than leave the scene. This thing pushing you into the right direction is not one of the two instincts; it is something else.[35] It is the moral conscience overriding your instinct for self-preservation and prompting you to do the right thing, even at the risk of your life.

The moral law code evident in all individuals is not simply natural instinct. The moral law code is acknowledged by all individuals. It is evident in all cultures, is undeniable, and is more than our instinct. A universal moral law derives its source from a sovereign lawgiver who is a personal and morally good being.

Conclusion

The fact that the universe has a beginning, that it displays evidence of design, and that there is a universal moral law presents a compelling case for the existence of God. These arguments show that the worldview of naturalism cannot be true. They also demonstrate that the worldview of pantheism cannot be true.

One of my most delightful discussions about God was with a brilliant Hindu man at the University of Texas. He had three master's degrees in philosophy, engineering, and computer science. He was from India and born into the Brahman priest class, the highest class in

---

[35] Ibid., 22.

Hinduism. As a devout Hindu, he believed Brahma was an impersonal force made of all things in the universe. I explained to him the three classic arguments for the existence of God. He thought them through carefully and said that these were valid arguments I had presented. I then stated, "Pantheism cannot be true, for since the universe has a beginning, it cannot be eternal. Second, since the universe displays design, we must conclude there is intelligence behind its creation. Intelligence is tied to personhood. Third, there is a universal moral code. Morality is also tied to personhood, not to matter. Therefore, the creator must be a personal being, not an impersonal force." He looked at me and replied, "I never heard it presented that way before. I will think about this." We parted as friends. Through my honest discussions with him, I not only gained insight into Hindu beliefs, but his response also showed me the strengths and weaknesses of the evidence I laid out before him.

Since the worldviews of naturalism and pantheism are not true, the religions and ideologies built on the worldviews of naturalism and pantheism are ultimately false. Therefore, we are left with the worldview of theism. What remains are the theistic religions of Judaism, Islam, and Christianity. If God exists, miracles are possible. If there is a God, there can be acts of God. All three religions acknowledge that God confirms His message and messengers with acts of God, or miracles. We will examine which of these religions is confirmed by acts of God, thus demonstrating evidence of divine inspiration.

CHAPTER 3

See Darwin's Dilemma

D id Darwin's theory conclusively prove that God does not exist? Darwin's theory remains one of the most influential theories of our time in areas that reach beyond science. This theory has become an all-embracing meta-narrative of the culture. His theory is taught as the only viable theory explaining the origin and diversity of life. Darwin's theory attempts to explain that all life began as the result of natural processes with no supernatural intervention by a creator.

Biologist William Provine from Cornell University asserts that Darwinism is a comprehensive philosophy stating that all life can be explained by natural causes acting randomly, which implies no need for a creator. Furthermore, if God did not create the world, the entire body of Christian belief collapses.[1] In other words, if Darwin's theory is true, the universe and life are the result of a cosmic accident. Provine further states that Darwinism ultimately means that there is "no life after death, no ultimate foundation for ethics, no ultimate meaning for life, no free will."[2]

It is vitally important to understand that Darwin's theory remains exactly that: a theory. Although many teach it as fact, it remains a theory. Granted, it is taught as the only viable theory explaining the

---

[1]   Charles Colson, *How Now Shall We Live?* (Wheaton, IL.: Tyndale House Publishers, 1999), 91.

[2]   Ibid., 92.

origin and diversity of life, and any criticism against it is met with very strong reactions. However, Darwin's theory has failed to present a conclusive case for the origin and diversity of life. It remains a theory but with several significant flaws. Hundreds of scientists today acknowledge the shortcomings of Darwin's theory and believe that an intelligent designer is a more reasonable explanation for the origin and design discovered in the universe.

There are several key flaws in Darwin's theory. I will present a brief overview of a few. However, for more extensive treatments and detailed presentations, I strongly recommend the work of top scientists, such as Michael Behe, Francis Collins, Bill Dembsky, Robert Jastrow, Stephen Meyer, Hugh Ross, Jonathan Wells, and works from scientific organizations such as the Discovery Institute and the Institute of Creation Research.

Darwin's Fatal Flaws

Missing Mechanism for Macroevolutionary Change

As we approach this topic, we must understand two key terms: microevolution and macroevolution. Microevolution refers to minor variations that occur within a species over time. For example, the breeding of different types of dogs is a form of microevolution. We all agree microevolutionary change does occur. Macroevolution, however, refers to the emergence of major innovations or the unguided development of new structures, such as wings; new organs, such as lungs; and new body plans, such as the origins of insects and birds. Macroevolutionary changes also include those changes above the species level, especially those of new phyla or classes.

One of the key flaws in Darwin's theory is that it is missing the mechanism for macroevolutionary change. Unfortunately, in many presentations, microevolutionary examples are used to prove Darwinian evolution. However, to prove Darwin's theory, one must show that natural causes can create macroevolutionary change.

Darwinists teach that, given enough time, natural selection and mutations can create macroevolutionary changes. However, these two fail to produce such changes. It has been shown that natural selection preserves the strongest within a species but is not a force that changes it. One example that is often used is the peppered moth. In this example, there are two moths: a white moth and a dark moth. Before industrialization, the white moth was well camouflaged in the white bark of the trees, and the dark moths were picked off by the birds because they were exposed. However, once industrialization took place, soot turned the trees to a dark color. As a result, the white moths were now exposed, and the dark moths were now more suited to survive. The problem with this example is that no macroevolutionary change has occurred. We still have a moth. No new body parts or organs were created.

The second mechanism for macroevolutionary changes is mutations. Darwinists propose that mutations occur that create small variations in species, and over time, they eventually lead to the formation of a new species. However, mutations also fail to account for macroevolutionary changes. First, the vast majority of mutations are harmful. Award-winning neonatologist Dr. Reginald Tsang writes:

I have been a neonatologist-pediatrician for over 30 years, and I have seen hundreds of mutation affected infants, and read about thousands more in the medical literature. And I have never seen a real live "good" mutation. In fact, the medical literature is full of reports showing how even a small one amino acid mistake/mutation in the phenomenally complex DNA can cause a profound problem. So how is it the biologist, who has never seen a single human patient with mutation, can claim, or "fantasize", that mutation is the essence of evolution, which propels organisms to increasing complexity and "advance" to a "higher" species. ... Sorry, sci-fi folks, this NEVER happens. The word "mutation" in real life is a terror loaded word. We pediatricians say the word softly, quietly, and carefully, and try very hard to use other words around it to "soften" the deadly blow that the mother will sense immediately. No, Alice, there are no good mutations in real life. Maybe in Wonderland.[3]

---

[3] Reginald Tsang, "Congratulations, Your Baby Has a Mutation?" *Science and Faith*, Volume 1 Issue 2, December 2006.

The majority of mutations are harmful. In practical sciences like medicine, a mutation is a disaster. However, in Darwinian evolution, we suddenly are presented with a theory that asserts that hundreds of beneficial mutations occurred which caused beneficial new parts to appear, thereby creating a new species. This goes against the findings of medical research according to men such as Dr. Tsang.

We also know that the gene pool has limits for variation. Biologist Ray Bohlin writes, "Theoretically, it may seem difficult to propose that immense variety can occur within a group of organisms while at the same time this variety is constrained within certain genetically induced limits. It may even seem contradictory. But in the intervening years, my belief in the proposal has only strengthened, and my confidence in any evolutionary mechanism to accomplish significant adaptational change has waned considerably."[4]

Using the example of the breeding of dogs, we know that the breeding of domesticated animals has not produced a new species. Natural selection prevents the appearance of extreme variation that human breeders like to produce. When domesticated animals return to the wild, the succeeding generations revert to the original wild type, and highly specialized breeds disappear. Breeding also shows there is a limit as to how far a species can mutate. We know we have reached the limits because the new breeds begin to have too many deficiencies in their system to make them a strong breed of dog. Mutations cause small changes, but for Darwin's theory, we must prove they create large beneficial changes.

One famous example used by Darwinists is the famous drosophila fruit fly experiment. In this experiment, fruit flies were exposed to various amounts of radiation. What resulted was a strange assortment of fruit flies. Some had tiny wings, some had crumpled wings, some had large eyes, and others had dark bodies and other variations. Most of the mutations were harmful. The major shortcoming is that the drosophila fruit fly was still just a fruit fly! No new body parts had been created.

One of the key flaws in Darwin's theory is the failure to produce a mechanism for macroevolutionary change. The two mechanisms of

---

[4] Ray Bohlin, *Creation, Evolution, and Modern Science* (Grand Rapids, MI.: Kregel Publications, 2000), 36.

natural selection and mutations have failed to demonstrate that they can produce macroevolutionary change. This presents a fatal flaw in Darwin's theory.

The Fossil Record

Darwinism has failed to produce a mechanism for macroevolutionary change. A second flaw is in the fossil record. According to Darwin's theory, we should have found his tree of life in the fossil record. In other words we should find fossils showing the step-by-step progression beginning with a common ancestor, a simple one-celled organism, then later fossils slowly developing into complex life forms thus forming a tree-like pattern, starting with a one-celled organism and then developing branches of diverse life forms. Instead of this gradual progression, we have an explosion of life forms appearing suddenly during the Cambrian Explosion, and the species that appeared remained virtually unchanged from their original form.

The Cambrian Explosion occurred between six hundred million and five hundred million years ago, and this poses a serious challenge to Darwin's theory. Instead of seeing a gradual progression beginning with a few species that evolve into more complex species, there is a sudden appearance of many fully-formed phyla and classes of animals. The Cambrian Explosion reveals that the highest levels of the biological hierarchy appear right from the beginning![5]

The Precambrian fossils consisted of single-celled organisms. They did not provide the record of gradual progression needed to support Darwin's theory.[6] Evolutionary theorist Jeffrey Schwartz wrote that the major animal groups "appear in the fossil record as Athena did from the head of Zeus—full-blown and raring to go."[7] The fossil record further reveals that forms go extinct or stabilize. The most prevailing characteristic of fossil species is stasis; there is little change in fossils from the Cambrian explosion.

---

[5]   Jonathan Wells, *Icons of Evolution* (Washington D.C.: Regenery Publishing, 2000), 35.

[6]   Ibid., 38.

[7]   Ibid., 41.

Equally baffling to the Darwinists is the lack of transitional forms in the fossil record. There should be thousands of transitional fossils that show fish transitioning into amphibians, amphibians transitioning into land-walking reptiles, and reptiles transitioning into mammals. However, there are very few fossils that would qualify as a transitional form. Darwin himself expected to find numerous transitional forms in the fossil record. He stated,

> The number of intermediate varieties, which have formerly existed, [must] be truly enormous. Why then is not every geological formation and every stratum full of such intermediate links? Geology assuredly does not reveal any such finely graduated organic chain; and this perhaps, is the most obvious and serious objection which can be urged against the theory.[8]

Darwin felt the fossil record was incomplete but was hopeful that future discoveries would reveal the transitional forms. However, even after the discovery of thousands of fossils, we have not found an abundance of transitional forms showing Darwin's progression. Thus, alternate forms of Darwin's theory, such as Stephen J. Gould's Punctuated Equilibrium, have been presented to account for this significant gap in the theory.

According to Darwin's theory, small mutations occurred in a species that eventually led to the development of new body parts creating a new species. What we should expect in the fossil record is then numerous transitional forms that show this process. One such example is the evolution of the rodent into the bat. If Darwin's theory is true, we should expect to find numerous transitional forms showing this progression. We should find numerous rodents with stubs on their sides. We should then see these stubs gradually extending and growing in the fossils that follow until we arrive at the modern bat. In other words, the first generation should be rodents with stubs followed by a second generation of rodents with small wing-like projections that grow longer and longer to evolve into the modern bat. However, we

---

[8]   Charles Darwin, *The Origin of Species* (New York: Collier Books, 1962), 308.

do not have this in the fossil record. What we have instead is a rodent and then fully developed bats. We are missing these intermediate forms.

Another problem is that mutations and natural selection are supposed to be the mechanisms for macroevolutionary change. However, we must ask what benefit is 25 percent or 50 percent of a wing for a rodent? The wing at this stage is too small to allow the rodent to fly, but too big to allow the rodent to be mobile on the ground. How would this be a beneficial mutation, and how would this be a beneficial trait that would be passed on through natural selection? The fossil record goes against Darwin's progression, and his only mechanisms for macroevolutionary change work against his theory.

As previously stated, there are very few, if any, transitional forms in the fossil record. One hopeful candidate was Archaeopteryx, an ancient reptile-like bird that was discovered in 1861. This "link" between reptiles and birds was heralded by Darwinists as proof of transitional forms. However, paleontologists today do not consider Archaeopteryx a transitional form but rather the earliest known member of an extinct group of birds.[9] However, even if we grant Archaeopteryx the status of a reptile-bird, Darwinists still have a dilemma. There still needs to be numerous transitional forms between reptiles and Archaeopteryx. In other words, where are the ancestors of Archaeopteryx? According to paleontologists, the most likely ancestor of Archaeopteryx is Compsognathus, a bird-like dinosaur. However, Compsognathus appears long after Archaeopteryx.[10] Archaeopteryx remains an interesting animal, but it fails to fill the gap between reptiles and birds.

Philip Johnson summarizes the testimony of the fossil record. The history of most fossil species includes two features particularly inconsistent with gradualism:

1. Stasis: Most species exhibit no directional change during their tenure on earth. They appear in the fossil record looking pretty much the same as when they disappear; morphological change is usually limited and directionless.

---

[9]   Wells, 116.
[10]   Ibid., 120.

2. Sudden appearance. In any local area, a species does not arise gradually by the steady transformation of its ancestors; it appears all at once and "fully formed."[11]

The fossil record goes against Darwin's theory instead of proving it. Instead, the fossil record appears to fit the biblical account which states that God created each of the creatures fully formed and according to "its kind," (Genesis 1:21–25) where *kind* in this context refers to "species".[12]

The Origin of Life

One final flaw in Darwin's theory is that it fails to explain how life came from nonlife. Darwinists present the hypothesis that as the earth was forming, there developed a primordial soup. This primordial soup was somehow ignited by an electrical current of energy producing amino acids, which are the building blocks of proteins necessary for life.

The famous Miller–Urey Experiment is often presented as proof for this hypothesis. In the 1950s, Stanley Miller and Harold Urey performed their experiment to prove the beginning of life. Urey believed the earth's early atmosphere consisted primarily of hydrogen, methane, ammonia, and water vapor. Miller made a closed gas apparatus connecting a flask of water, a chamber for his gases and electrodes, a water condenser and a trap to collect the anticipated liquid. Miller pumped the air out of the chamber replacing the chamber with hydrogen, methane and ammonia. He heated water in the flask, and the vapor traveled up the airtight tubes into the chamber of gases where the electrodes set off sparks simulating electricity. After traveling through the chamber, the condenser cooled the gas combination creating a liquid that dripped into the trap. The resulting red water produced glycine and alanine, amino acids found in proteins. Many touted this as evidence that life can come from nonliving matter.

11 Philip Johnson, *Darwin on Trial* (Downers Grove, IL.: InterVarsity Press, 1991), 50.

12 Francis Brown, S.R. Driver, and Charles Briggs, *The Brown-Driver-Briggs Hebrew and English Lexicon* (Peabody, MA.: Hendrickson Publishers, 1979), 569.

However, major flaws were discovered in the experiment. Urey assumed the earth's atmosphere had the same composition as interstellar gas clouds. Scientists, however, concluded that the earth's atmosphere was formed by gases released from volcanoes. Volcanoes release water vapor, carbon dioxide, nitrogen, and hydrogen. If the principal ingredient in the atmosphere was water vapor, then the atmosphere contained oxygen, for as radiation splits hydrogen from the oxygen, it leaves oxygen in the atmosphere. Since hydrogen is too light for the earth's gravity to hold, it would have escaped from the atmosphere. Without the hydrogen, methane and ammonia could not have been major components of the earth's atmosphere. Therefore, the earth's atmosphere contained oxygen and was different from the atmosphere of the Miller-Urey experiment. The Miller -Urey experiment was repeated; only this time an atmosphere of water vapor, carbon dioxide, and nitrogen was created. When electrodes produced sparks simulating lightning in the gas chamber, this experiment produced no amino acids at all. Modern experiments have failed to produce any substantive results.[13]

Darwin's theory is promoted as the only viable explanation for the origin of life, yet scientists have failed to explain or demonstrate how life came from nonlife. Continued years of research have only led to more difficulties, obstacles, and eventually dead ends. Scientist Fazale Rana summarizes the disappointing results after decades of research:

> Their research seemed to turn up more dead ends than fruitful avenues to study. They also started probing the geochemical and fossil records of Earth's earliest rocks—data that establish time constraints for beginning of life scenarios. In addition, researchers began applying information theory to the origin-of-life dilemma and started to understand life's minimal complexity. Problems grew increasingly insurmountable. The thrills of early decades of research gave way to growing frustration and pessimism.[14]

---

[13] Fazale Rana & Hugh Ross, *Origins of Life* (Colorado Springs, CO.: NavPress, 2004), 99-101.

[14] Fazal Rana and Hugh Ross, 25.

Scientist now are abandoning long-held naturalistic theories of a prebiotic soup and are postulating that life was transported to earth by another life-form from another planet. However, even if we could discover that life arrived from another planet, we would still have to answer the question, "How did *that* life-form develop?"

Nobel Prize-winning physiologist George Wald concluded in his later years that the most reasonable conclusion is that a preexisting intelligence created a universe capable of producing life. "It is a mind that has composed a physical universe that breeds life, and so eventually evolves creatures that know and create: science, art, and technology-making creatures."[15] Antony Flew, this generation's greatest atheist philosopher, became a theist because he saw there was no evidence to support Darwin's theory that life came from nonlife. He concluded, "The only satisfactory explanation for the origin of such end-directed, self-replicating life as we see on earth is an infinitely intelligent Mind."[16]

The most reasonable explanation for the origin of life is an intelligent creator. Darwin has not shown that natural causes can somehow create life.

Conclusion

This is just a brief overview of some of the major flaws of Darwin's theory. Despite these fatal flaws, it is still presented in schools and universities throughout the world as the only viable explanation for the origin and diversity of life. However, Darwin's theory lacks the supporting evidence to uphold its premises. Therefore, Darwin's theory has major shortcomings and has not refuted the evidence for the existence of God.

Darwinism fails to explain how the universe came into existence, how the laws of nature came to be, how life originated, and how we arrived at such complexity and diversity of life. As we discover more in the sciences, the case against Darwinism grows, and the case for an intelligent creator continues to develop.

---

[15] Antony Flew, *There is no a God: How the World's Most Notorious Atheist Changed His Mind* (New York: Harper One, 2007), 132.

[16] Flew, 132.

CHAPTER 4

See the Truth on Truth

I s truth relative or absolute? Is there such a thing as universal and objective truth?

Can any group or individual honestly say they possess the truth? The prevalent view in the culture today is that truth is relative. Christianity, on the other hand, is built on the premise that truth is absolute, and that the teachings of the Bible are universal. The notion that truth is relative presents one of the most significant challenges facing the Christian faith.

A survey of the American public revealed that 66 percent agreed with the statement, "There is no such thing as absolute truth."[1] Among youth, 70 percent believe that there is no such thing as absolute truth; two people could define "truth" in conflicting ways and both would be correct."[2] Relativism has made significant inroads into the church as well. According to the latest research, 53 percent of adults in church believe there is no absolute truth. Among youth in church, research shows that 57 percent do not believe that an objective standard of truth exists.[3] For two millennia, the Church has been the guardian of truth and cannot

---

[1] Gene Edward Veith, *Postmodern Times,* (Wheaton, IL: Crossway Books, 1994), 16.
[2] Barna, *Third Millenium Teens,* (Ventura, CA.: Barna Research Group, 1999), 44.
[3] Josh McDowell and Bob Hostetler, *The New Tolerance* (Wheaton, IL.: Tyndale House Publishers, 1998) 172-173.

allow its foundation to be dismantled by relativism. It is important that Christians understand the nature of truth and engage relativist thinking.

Absolute Truth

Truth that is defined as being absolute possesses the following qualities:[4]

- Truth is discovered, not invented.
- Truth is transcultural; it can be conveyed across different cultures.
- Truth is unchanging; it can be conveyed across time.
- Beliefs cannot change a truth statement no matter how sincere one may be.
- Truth is unaffected by the attitude of the one professing it.
- All Truths are absolute.
- Truth is knowable.

In order for truth to be absolute and hold these qualities, it must be grounded in a source that is personal, unchanging, and sovereign over all creation.

Relativism

The popular view on truth in our culture today is that truth is relative. Postmodern relativists build their understanding of truth on the foundation of the naturalist worldview. Truth then has its origin in man. This leads to conclusions that differ greatly from those who hold to absolute truth. Relativists believe:

- Truth is created, not discovered. Truth is a matter of perspective, and each culture or individual defines for themselves what is truth.
- Since truth is invented, there is no universal transcultural truth. Cultures or individuals will define truth differently according to their background and perspective.
- Truth changes since it is inseparably connected to individuals and cultures. Since individuals and cultures continually change, truth perpetually changes.

---

[4] Norman Geisler and Frank Turek, *I Don't Have Enough Faith to be an Atheist* (Wheaton, IL.: Crossway Books, 2004), 37-38.

- Since truth is a matter of a group or individual's perspective, one's beliefs can change a truth statement.
- Since an individual determines truth, truth is affected by the attitude of the one professing it.
- There can be no such thing as absolute truth.
- Absolute truth is not knowable. Absolute objective truth cannot be known since it is built on the shifting foundation of man's perceptions. Because each individual's perception is different, truth cannot be known.

Jim Leffel, Director of the Crossroads Project, an apologetics ministry designed to equip Christians to understand and effectively communicate to our postmodern culture, summarizes postmodern relativism as follows.

> Relativism says the truth isn't fixed by outside reality, but is instead decided by a group or individual for themselves. Truth isn't discovered; it is manufactured. Truth is ever changing not only in insignificant matters of taste or fashion but also in crucial matters of spirituality, morality, and reality itself.[5]

Leading postmodern thinker John Caputo writes, "The cold, hermeneutic truth is that there is no truth, no master name which holds things captive."[6] Both men summarize the postmodern belief that objective truth does not exist leading to the conclusion that all truth claims are equal even if they are contradictory.

Here are some common objections regarding truth:

- There are no absolutes. All truth is relative.
- Truth is what each individual perceives it to be.

---

[5] Jim Leffel, "Our New Challenge: Postmodernism" in *The Death of Truth*, ed. Dennis McCallum, (Minneapolis: Bethany House Publishers, 1996), 31.

[6] John Caputo, *Radical Hermeneutics: Repetition, Deconstruction, and the Hermeneutic Project* (Bloomington, IN: Indiana University Press, 1987), 192, quoted in Josh McDowell, *The New Evidence That Demands a Verdict* (Nashville, TN.: Thomas Nelson Publishers, 1999), 616

- Man uses reason to determine truth, but our reasoning ability is limited and thus cannot determine truth.
- Language is flawed and cannot communicate perfectly. Since truth is communicated by the flawed vehicle of language, truth cannot be known.
- Each individual has a different perspective; therefore, each person perceives truth differently. Since no one perceives reality perfectly, no one can have the truth.

These appear to be formidable challenges. Is truth relative or absolute? Can we answer these challenges? In the following sections, I will explain why relativism fails and expand upon the truth on truth.

Relativism's Slippery Slide

The philosophy of relativism should be rejected for several reasons. First, relativism fails because it is a self-defeating position. A self-defeating statement is one that fails its own standard; it contradicts itself or applies the very premise it denies to make its case. Therefore, to say, "There are no absolute truths," is, indeed, an absolute truth statement. To say, "There is no truth," is a statement of truth. When a relativist says, "All truth is relative," we need to ask him, "Is that a relative statement?" If it is, why should we take his statement seriously? When a relativist claims that all truth is relative and believes that all should hold this principle, he just made an absolute truth statement. To say, "There is no truth" requires one to acknowledge a truth statement. The truth that there is no truth is self-defeating. Truth does exist and is undeniable.

Second, relativism fails because it is not livable. If truth were relative, no one would be wrong about anything. If truth is whatever I perceive it to be, I would not be wrong about anything. However, each day we acknowledge absolute truth and identify error. Without doing so, we could not function in the real world. This would not be possible if truth were relative.

For example we acknowledge that 2+2 = 4. We acknowledge this and other mathematical truths each day. If we did not, we could not have math, engineering, science, or an economic system. When I go to the doctor, I expect him to communicate absolute truth to me. If he says, "Today you have high blood pressure, and you need to take medication," I expect his assessment to correspond with the facts. If I do not think he is right, I get a second opinion to test his results. Thus, I am assuming there is absolute truth by which I can measure the accuracy of his statement.

Third, relativism is built on the naturalist worldview. Relativism is a logical conclusion if God does not exist and truth derives its source from man, for man does not have perfect perception of reality. Man is finite and limited in his knowledge. Therefore, if truth derives its origin in man, it would be changing and different for each individual. However, the evidence indicates we live in a theistic universe. Truth does not derive its source from man but from God, whose very nature is truth. God created a universe founded on His truth, and He created beings who are capable of discovering and receiving His truth. His truth is what established the world, and it is His truth that we are designed to live by.

Finally, language can communicate objective truth. Based on the naturalist worldview, postmodern relativists believe language originates with man and that communication is confined within the context of a person's particular culture. They then conclude that language cannot convey objective truth. However, language originates with God and is intrinsic to His personality and nature. Through His Word, He created the universe (Genesis 1:3 and John 1:1). All creation finds its origin in God's Word. Mankind uses language because we are created in God's image. It is through language that God creates and maintains a relationship with man.

Granted, there is a difference between the language of God and human language. Human language is fallen and, therefore, limited. However, God continues to communicate with humans through language found in His Word and through His Son. In contrast, postmodern relativists view language as a prison house since it is a cultural construct with no transcendent meaning outside the text. This is true if God does not exist. Human language may have gaps and limits, but it is an overstatement to say language cannot communicate objective truth. Veith states,

Human language is a sign, a trace, of a divine language. Language may get in the way sometimes, but it is revelatory. Meaning is not only subjective; the external world is itself grounded in the Word of God, which established its form and gave it an objective meaning. When we study science, we are not merely making up mental models, but we are, in a sense, reading the divine language inscribed in the universe. Language is not merely a prison house; God's language can break in from the outside and give us freedom.[7]

The world is built on God's word, which encompasses meaning and objective truth. God has ordained language, and although human language is flawed, it is rooted in His being and can indeed communicate truths about His world. Truth exists outside of language; it exists in the mind of God.

We communicate truth using language, and we do so each day. I was once speaking at a university in North Carolina when a doctoral student objected to my presentation and said, "There is no such thing as absolute truth because language cannot communicate truth. Language is flawed. We perceive words differently, so we cannot communicate truth through language." I then repeated his words to him, "Language cannot communicate truth." He acknowledged his statement. I then asked him, "Is that a true statement you made?" He then paused and reflected on his words. I then asked him, "Didn't you just use language to communicate that truth?" He suddenly realized the he had made a self-defeating statement, smiled, and changed the subject.

How Truth is Discovered

How does one come to discover truth? Truth is discovered with self-evident laws of logic called First Principles. Two key principles are the Law of Noncontradiction and the Law of the Excluded Middle.

The Law of Noncontradiction states that two opposite statements cannot both be true at the same time in the same sense.[8] For example,

---

[7] Gene Edward Veith, *Postmodern Times* (Wheaton, IL.: Crossway Books, 1994), 67–68.

[8] Norman Geisler and Ron Brooks, *When Skeptics Ask* (Wheaton, IL.: Victor Books, 1990), 271.

if we make the statement "God exists," its opposite, "God does not exist," cannot be true at the same time. If one is true, the other must be false. Humans are designed so that we cannot believe contradictory propositions.

This is a universal law that cannot be refuted. Any truth statement requires that its converse cannot be true. Postmodern relativists and pantheists will often state that they reject this law, but that is not the same as actually refuting the law. Those who make the appeal that the Law of Non-Contradiction does not apply to religion or morality make a statement of truth that cannot be contradicted. In order to refute the law, they must appeal to the law itself. Philosophy of Religion professor Harold Netland states, "Any meaningful affirmation about anything at all, regardless of how cryptic, vague, paradoxical or imprecise the statement might be, if intended as true, makes implicit appeal to the principle ruling out its negation as false."[9]

The second law is the Law of the Excluded Middle, which states that something either is or is not; there is no third alternative.[10] The statement "God exists" is either true or false. There is no third choice.

Not only do we use the First Principles to discover truth, we also use our senses to observe the world around us. From these observations, we draw conclusions. This process of discovery is called *induction*. Through logic and observation, we can make conclusions that are reasonably certain but not always absolutely certain. For example, we can be reasonably sure that the sun will rise and set tomorrow. We cannot be absolutely sure since we do not have perfect knowledge of the future. However, we act on our reasonably sure knowledge and make our plans. Although we may not have absolute certainty, we can discover truth and make conclusions that can be trusted.

Postmodern relativists overstate their case when they say truth cannot be known. Truth is undeniable, objective, and absolute. Truth is also narrow since its opposite is false.

---

[9]   Harold Netland, *Encountering Religious Pluralism* (Downers Grove, IL.: InterVarsity Press, 2001), 296.

[10]   Geisler and Turek, *I Don't Have Enough Faith to be an Atheist* (Wheaton, IL.: Crossway Books, 2004), 62.

What is Truth?

Truth is defined as that which corresponds to its object or that which describes an actual state of affairs.[11] Truth then is what corresponds to reality. Truth is absolute and narrow by nature because it excludes its opposite. Although relativists will argue that we cannot truly know reality, this is an exaggerated and inconsistent premise. One must know reality to be able to question the nature of one's reality.

We also live in a theistic universe with a God who is involved and understands the character of His creation. Therefore, what He says about His creation is true and authoritative. God has created man in His image with the ability to understand truth and to know reality. The correspondence theory is supported in the Old and New Testament.

The Old Testament Definition of Truth

The Hebrew word for truth is *emet* and involves ideas of support and stability. From this root, we derive a twofold notion of truth as "faithfulness" and "conformity to fact."[12] *Emet* can also mean that which is conformed to reality in contrast to anything that would be erroneous or deceitful. *Emet* can also connote that which is authentic, reliable, or simply right.[13]

The New Testament Definition

The New Testament word for truth is *aletheia* and retains the Hebrew idea of truth. Truth is defined as "conformity to fact." It also carries with it the ideas of genuineness and opposition to falsities. John, in his gospel, develops his unique meaning where truth refers to the reality of God the Father as revealed in Jesus the Son. John's understanding of truth presupposes a correspondence view of truth, but it also builds this foundation theologically by adding specific

---

[11] Ibid., 37.

[12] Roger Nicole, "The Biblical Concept of Truth" in *Scripture and Truth*, ed. D.A. Carson and John Woodridge, (Grand Rapids, MI.: Zondervan, 1983), 290 quoted in Douglas Groothuis, *Truth Decay* (Downers Grove, Il.: 2000), 60.

[13] Ibid., 62.

content concerning the manifestation of truth in Jesus Christ (John 7:28 and 8:16).[14]

Both the Old and New Testaments emphasize that truth conforms to reality and is an antithesis to lies and errors. The biblical view of truth contains the idea of factuality, faithfulness, and completeness. Truth is not a cultural construct of the Jewish people or the Christians. God presented His truth to them, and they were expected to live in conformity to this truth.[15]

Truth is Revealed by God

Truth finds its source in God who is personal and moral. Paul states in Romans 1 and 2 that God has revealed Himself through creation and the human conscience. God has also unveiled Himself through the Bible, His special revelation. Second Timothy 3:16 states, "All Scripture is God-breathed and is useful for teaching, rebuking, correcting and training in righteousness ..." God, whose nature is truth, communicates His truth through language that has eternally existed with God. He uses this language to convey truth to creatures created in His image.

Objective Truth Exists and is Knowable

Objective truth is truth that is not dependent on the perspective or attitudes of any individual. God's truth is objective because truth is rooted in the nature of God, who is truth. He is the source of truth, and His truths are true regardless of what the beliefs or attitudes an individual or culture may have toward it. Those who do not acknowledge God's truth will be judged by it. God is just to judge people because His truth is objective and knowable. Consequently, all are accountable to respond to it.

---

[14] D.M. Crump, "Truth" in *Dictionary of Jesus and the Gospels*, ed. Joel Green, Scott Mcknight, and I Howard Marshall (Downers Grove, Il.: InterVarsity Press, 1992), 859, quoted in Douglas Groothuis, *Truth Decay* (Downers Grove, Il.: 2000), 63.

[15] Groothuis, 64.

Biblical Truth is Absolute

God's truth is absolute. This means that God's truth is true without exception and does not change. Beliefs change, but truth itself is unchangeable. God is the author of absolute truth because He is eternal and His character does not change.

Truth is Universal

God's truth applies to all peoples and all cultures at all times because He is ruler over all creation (Philippians 2:6). His authority and truths apply to every area. In the Great Commission, Jesus states, "All authority in heaven and earth has been given to me. Go into all the world and make disciples, teaching them to obey all that I have commanded you." (Matthew 28:20) In the Great Commission, Jesus declares His rule over all creation. The authority of His laws extends to all and must be obeyed by all people.

Truth is Eternal

Isaiah 40:8 states, "The grass withers and the flower falls, but the word of God endures forever." God's truth is rooted in His eternal nature. What was true two thousand years ago remains true to this day. The application of truth will change, but the truth itself endures forever.

Truth is Exclusive

Truth is narrow and exclusive since whatever it opposes is false. God states in Isaiah 43:10, "Before me no god was formed, nor will there be one after me." God is saying He alone is God, and there are no other gods. Worship of any other divine being is an act of living in falsehood. Truth is precise and without deviation. The Law of Noncontradiction states that two opposite statements cannot be true at the same time in the same sense. If God states He alone is God, polytheism cannot be true at the same time. The Law of Noncontradiction is a universal law because God's truth is exclusive and narrow.

Truth is Coherent

All truth statements are coherent and consistent with one another. "In a universe subject to the rule of one creator-God ... truth is seen as an interrelated and coherent whole."[16] It is not God's nature to teach what is contradictory, illogical, or false. Therefore, truth statements will not contradict one another.

Engaging Relativism

It can be a frustrating experience when entering into a discussion with a relativist, for as soon as one begins to present truth, he or she will immediately declare, "There is no such thing as absolute truth." That often ends the discussion. However, the failure of relativism can be exposed by turning a relativist's statement back on itself and revealing the self-defeating nature of the argument. My professor Dr. Norman Geisler calls this the "Road Runner" technique. When this is done, the relativist realizes he has run off the cliff with no support for his premise. This is just like the *Road Runner* cartoon: The coyote chasing the road runner thinks he has the bird in his grasp when, suddenly, the road runner stops. The coyote runs off the cliff, realizing that his feet are dangling in midair.

For example, when a relativist states, "There are no absolutes," the self-refuting claim can be exposed by turning the sentence back on itself and asking, "Is that an absolute truth statement?" Thus, the self-refuting nature of that claim is demonstrated. When a relativist states, "There is no such thing as truth," one can simply ask him, "Is that a true statement?"

I was in Chicago one summer speaking to college students. At the end of my first session, a student named Gordon stood up and angrily stated, "I don't believe a word you said. Christianity cannot be true because there is no such thing as absolute truth. Truth is relative." I then asked Gordon, "There is no such thing as absolute truth. Is that an absolute truth?" He started shaking, and then said, "I can't stand Christians because Christians judge other people who disagree with them." I asked Gordon, "Is it wrong for all people to falsely judge others of different beliefs?" He said "Absolutely!" I then pointed out to Gordon, "That is another absolute: It is wrong for all people to judge

---

[16] Arthur Holmes, *All Truth Is God's Truth* (Grand Rapids, MI.: Eerdmans Publishing, 1977), 7, quoted in Doug Groothius, *Truth Decay* (Downers Grove, IL.: InterVarsity Press, 2000), 80.

others falsely." He then was visibly trembling now and said, "I can't stand Christians because they hate homosexuals, and that is wrong!" I then asked Gordon, "Is it wrong for people to hate others who live a different lifestyle?" He said, "Yes, it is wrong for all people to do that." I then stated, "That is another absolute: It is wrong to hate others of a different lifestyle. We went from no absolutes to three!"

Gordon stood silent, pondering what had just happened. I then offered to meet with him over coffee later that night. He came to me at the coffee break, and this time his spirit was totally different. He sat down calmly and asked, "Can I ask you one final question?" I said, "Sure, Gordon." He then asked, "If God is so smart, if He knew man would sin and create all these problems, why did God create man in the first place?" I smiled because he had just walked into a presentation of the Gospel. That night, I got to share the Gospel message with him.

Learning to turn a relativist's statement back on itself quickly and gently exposes the self-defeating nature of the relativist statement.

Conclusion

The Bible, together with human logic and experience, supports the notion that truth is absolute and not relative. Truth is narrow since it rejects its opposite. It is universal, unchanging, and knowable. Absolute truth finds its source in God who is eternal, unchanging, and sovereign over all creation. God, who is truth, communicates truth to beings made in His image. Relativism should be rejected because the evidence shows we live in a theistic universe. Since the worldview of naturalism is false, the foundation upon which relativists build is unsound. Relativism is also self-defeating, unlivable, and contrary to biblical teaching.

CHAPTER 5

See the Case for Miracles

I was a guest on a radio show fielding questions from listeners. Questions ranged from evidence for God to Buddhism. In the middle of the show, one of the co-hosts posed a question that I am sure many Christians continue to wrestle with. Martin stated, "Pat, I believe in God, and the evidence you are giving is very good. However, I still struggle with miracles in the Bible. I feel I need to jettison my brain out the window in order to believe in miracles. Do I need to check my brains at the door in order to believe in miracles?" Skeptics doubt the possibility of miracles and Christians such as Martin struggle with this issue as well. Is it reasonable to believe in miracles?

Skeptics question the credibility of any miracle claim because many hold to a naturalistic worldview and believe that we live in a closed system in which the laws of nature are constant and cannot be violated. Therefore, there can be no such thing as a miracle. Theists believe that God confirms His message and His messengers with miracles. Miracles, specifically the miracles of Christ and His resurrection, confirm Christianity to be true. Without miracles, there can be no Son of God, no Word of God, and no hope of eternal life. Is there evidence for miracles? Can modern man believe in miracles?

What is a Miracle?

Some say that the birth of a baby is a miracle or that every sunset is a miracle. Many have even jokingly commented that my college graduation is a miracle. Although these events are special, they should not be considered miracles. Rather, these are examples of God working through the natural order of creation, or the laws of nature, that He has set in place.

In contrast, a miracle is a special act of God that interrupts the natural course of events. Natural laws describe what occurs regularly by natural causes, but miracles describe what happens rarely by supernatural causes. A miracle is an act of God designed to confirm the Word of God through a messenger of God.[1] A miracle is an event in which God temporarily makes an exception to the natural order of things to show that He is acting.[2] Miracles are unusual, irregular, and specific acts of God.

Several words are used for miracle in the Gospels. Dwight Pentecost defines the terms used in the New Testament:[3]

1. *Teras* occurs sixteen times in the New Testament and never appears alone but is used in combination with *semeion* or "signs." It stresses the startling, imposing and amazement-waking aspect of the miracle.

2. *Dynamis* emphasizes the power revealed in the miracle and the spiritual energy behind it.

3. *Endoxos* emphasizes miracles as being works in which the glory of God and the Son is revealed.

4. *Paradoxos* is used only in Luke 5:26, and it is translated "remarkable things." It emphasizes that the miracle is contrary to the natural order of the world.

5. *Thaumasios* is used only in Matthew 21:15 and is used of something that provokes wonder.

---

[1] Norman Geisler and Frank Turek, *I Don't Have Enough Faith to be an* Atheist (Wheaton: Crossway Books, 2004), 201-2.

[2] Douglas Geivett and Gary Habbermas, *In Defense of Miracles*, (Downers Grove, IL.: InterVarsity Press, 1997), 62-63.

[3] Dwight Pentecost, *The Words and Works of Christ* (Grand Rapids: Zondervan Publishing, 1981), 117.

6. *Semeion* is used to point to the power or meaning behind the miracle.

The word most often used is the word *sign,* or in the Greek, *semeion.* It is used seventy-seven times in the New Testament and primarily in the Gospels, where it is used forty-eight times. The basic meaning of *semeion* is a sign by which one recognizes a particular person or thing and serves as an authenticating mark or token. When associated with the miraculous, it can indicate a miracle accomplished by divinity or a miracle-worker, which goes against the natural course of things.[4]

The terms used for miracle in the New Testament lead us to conclude that miracles are a unique and extraordinary event awakening wonder (*teras*), brought about by divine power (*dynamis*), accomplishing some practical and benevolent work (*ergon* and *endoxos*), and authenticating the message and messenger as coming from God (*semeion*).[5] However, there is greater meaning to miracles than just the events themselves.

It was understood that only God could perform true miracles. Since God would not associate with false teachings, He would not associate His miracles with Christ if Christ's claims were false. Miracles validated Jesus' claim to be the divine Son of God. Scripture often refers to the miracles of Jesus as "signs," which indicate that Jesus is the divine Messiah. His extraordinary claims were supernaturally confirmed. Not only did miracles affirm His claims, they provoked a response from those who witnessed them. The proper conclusion witnesses should have derived is that someone with the authority of God has come to initiate the coming of the Kingdom of God.

The Purpose of Miracles

God performs miracles with a definite purpose in mind. He does not use them for entertainment purposes, nor does He carry them out among those whose hearts have been proven to be resistant to His message. In Matthew 12, the Jewish leaders ask Jesus to perform

---

4   Collin Brown ed. *Dictionary of New Testament Theology* (Grand Rapids: Zondervan Publishing, 1986), 2:626, 629.

5   John Witmer, *Immanuel* (Nashville: Word Publishing, 1998), 97-98.

a miracle for them. Jesus would not answer their challenge with a miracle, for He knew their hearts were hardened and that they would not listen to His message even if He performed a miracle there. He had done several miracles already, and they still did not believe. He tells the Pharisees the only sign they will be given is the sign of Jonah, which was a prophecy of His death and resurrection.

The purpose of miracles is to confirm God's message and His messenger. The three major monotheistic religions affirm that miracles confirm a messenger of God. In the Old Testament, God confirmed His prophets with miracles. God used miracles to assure the Israelites of Moses' call as a prophet of God (Exodus 4). In First Kings 18, God confirmed Elijah and his message with miracles.

God also confirmed Jesus and the apostles with miracles. Miracles reinforced the Messianic claims of Christ. In Luke 7, when John's disciples questioned Jesus, He authenticated his messianic qualifications with His record of miracles. In John 3:1–2, Nicodemus saw Jesus as a prophet because of His miracles. When Peter addressed the crowd in Jerusalem at Pentecost, he pointed to the miracles of Christ as confirmation that Jesus was indeed the Messiah (Acts 2:22).

Miracles also validated the apostles authority and message. In Acts 2:43, the crowds were amazed at the miracles the apostles performed and, as a result, many came to believe their message. Hebrews 2 states that God confirmed Jesus and the apostles through miracles (Hebrews 2:3–4).

The *Quran*, the holy book of Islam, also states that miracles confirm the divine calling of a prophet. Sura 4:63–65 states that God's power is manifest through the miraculous works of the prophets. Throughout the *Quran*, the people ask Muhammad to perform a miracle, but he refuses. The only miracle he points to is the *Quran* (3:181–184, 4:153, 6:8–9). However, the *Quran* teaches that the Old Testament prophets Moses and Elijah performed miracles (23:45, 7:100–108, 116–119). It even teaches that Jesus did miracles (5:113). In the *Quran*, Jesus and the Old Testament prophets are confirmed by miracles, whereas Muhammad does not have a testimony of executing miracles.

Possibility of Miracles

Are miracles possible? If God exists, miracles are possible. If there is a God, there can be acts of God. If there is a being beyond the natural world, there can be supernatural events. There is strong evidence that indicates we live in a theistic universe. In Chapter Two, I demonstrated that there is compelling evidence for the existence of God. The facts that the universe has a beginning (cosmological argument), that the order and design in the universe points to an intelligent designer (teleological argument), and the existence of our moral intuition (moral argument) present a compelling case for the existence of God.

If God exists, miracles are not only possible, they are actual. This is exemplified by the fact that the greatest miracle has occurred: God created the universe out of nothing. If there is a God who acts, there can be acts of God. Moreover, if this miracle has already taken place, it is also reasonable to believe in other miracles, such as parting the sea, the ten plagues of Egypt, turning water to wine, a virgin birth, and resuscitating a dead individual. In a theistic universe, we can believe in miracles.

Characteristics of True Miracles

It is important to distinguish between true miracles and false miracles. Norman Geisler presents five dimensions of a true miracle: an unnatural dimension, a theological dimension, a moral dimension, a teleological dimension, and a doctrinal dimension.[6]

Miracles have an unusual character or unnatural dimension because they are supernatural events. A miracle is an unusual and irregular act of God that interrupts the natural course of events and goes against the course of natural laws.[7] Second, miracles have a theological dimension. Miracles presuppose that a theistic God exists and that He is capable of intervening in the universe He created. In other words, God, who created and sustains the universe, can intervene when He chooses to produce true miracles. Richard Purtill, Professor Emeritus of Philosophy at Western Washington University, states, "If for some reason we find that some apparently wonderful event can be accounted for by some

---

[6]   Norman Geisler, *Baker Encyclopedia of Apologetics*, 472.

[7]   Ibid., 450.

power less that the power of God, then we withhold the designation 'miracle.'"[8]

Third, miracles have a moral dimension. Miracles reflect the character of God and bring glory to God. God is a morally perfect being, and miracles reflect His moral character. The miracles He performs are good and reflect His goodness or justice. He does not produce miracles that are evil or lead people into false teachings. Fourth, miracles have a teleological dimension. The purpose or miracles is to glorify God. Fifth, miracles have a doctrinal dimension. They are used by God to confirm His message and messenger (Deuteronomy 18:22 and Hebrews 2:3–4).

Geisler also points out five distinguishing marks of a miracle: true miracles are an exception to natural law, they produce immediate results, they always bring glory to God, they bring good to the natural world, and they never fail.[9]

Arguments against Miracles

The most formidable arguments against miracles are from philosopher David Hume (1711–1776), who was born and reared in Edinburgh, Scotland and attended Edinburgh University. He is considered the father of modern skepticism and wrote some of the most formidable arguments against the existence of God and miracles. His arguments or modified versions of them are still used today to argue against the miracle accounts of Christ. Hume believed that Christianity could not be true because miracles are not possible. Since Christianity substantiates its claims to be the true faith with the testimony of miracles, Christianity builds its claims on a false premise. Regarding his argument Hume stated, "I flatter myself that I have discovered an argument ... which, if just, will, with the wise and learned, be an everlasting check to all kinds of superstitious delusion, and consequently will be useful as long as the world endures"[10] Did Hume refute the possibility of miracles? Let us examine his arguments.

---

[8]   Richard Purtill, "Defining Miracles," in Doug Geivett and Gary Habermas, *In Defense of Miracles* (Downers Grove, IL: InterVarsity Press, 1997), 64.

[9]   Norman Geisler, *Baker Encyclopedia of Christian Apologetics,* 472.

[10]   David Hume, *An Enquiry Concerning Human Understanding* (New York: Liberal Arts Press, 1957), 118.

Hume's Presupposition

Hume's argument is built on his belief in a naturalistic universe where there is no God who can intervene and the laws of the universe cannot be altered. However, the evidence indicates that we live in a theistic universe. The existence of God dismantles the foundational premise of Hume's argument.

Hume's Argument against Miracles

Hume's argument against miracles is summarized as follows:[11]

1. A miracle is by definition a rare occurrence.
2. Natural law is by definition a description of regular occurrence.
3. Evidence for the regular is always greater for the rare.
4. Wise individuals always base belief on the greater evidence.
5. Therefore, wise individuals should never believe in miracles.

Hume's first and second premises are valid. However, the third premise is not. The evidence for the regular is not always greater than the rare. Hume's mistake here is that he adds up the evidence against miracles but does not weigh the evidence. Hume assumes that since natural laws are rarely or never violated, one should assume naturalistic explanations and not consider the possibility of a miracle or that a rare event has occurred. Thus, any rare event can never have as much evidence as common events. Although Hume's conclusion is true most of the time, there are times when the evidence that a rare event has occurred is greater.

For example, the vast majority of times, an individual who falls four hundred feet off a rocky cliff will die. However, there is the possibility that the rare event could happen where someone may survive such a fall. In fact, I know a man who fell off a four-hundred-foot rocky cliff in Hawaii and survived. He is a high school classmate and is now an evangelist. According to Hume, we should not believe this because it is a rare and amazing event. The vast majority of times,

---

[11]   Norman Geisler, *Baker Encyclopedia of Christian Apologetics*, 457.

someone falling off a four-hundred-foot cliff will die. However, here the evidence for a rare event outweighs the evidence for the norm. There were numerous eyewitnesses and written accounts. Hume does not examine the evidence for a miracle account; he just assumes since there is more evidence for common events, they outweigh evidence for rare events like a miracle. A wise person will examine the evidence rather than assume in advance to know the experience is uniform. Hume's argument against miracles fails.

Hume's Argument of Self-Canceling Claims

Hume's second argument against miracles is that all religions use miracles to support their system, and that no miracle can be used to support a religious system if any contrary religious system has a miracle to support it. (Contraries cannot be true; they cancel each other out.) His argument is summarized as follows:

1. Miracle accounts abound in the various world religions.
2. All religious systems use miracles to support their claims.
3. Since the world's religions contradict one another, their miracle claims cancel one another out.
4. Therefore, no miracle can be used to support a religious system.

Hume falsely assumes all alleged miracle claims from all the religions are equal. However, not all religions have eyewitness accounts like Christianity. For example, the *Quran* does not include any miracle accounts performed by the prophet Muhammad.[12] Miracle accounts appear in the *Hadith* written 150 years after Muhammad. Historian A. N. Sherwin White documents in his work that it takes at least two to three generations after the death of the eyewitnesses for complete legends to develop.[13] The miracle accounts of Muhammad appear three generations after the lifetime of the eyewitnesses. In contrast, eyewitnesses

---

[12] Norman Geisler and Abdul Saleeb, *Answering Islam* (Grand Rapids, MI.: Baker Books, 2002), 164.
[13] A. N. Sherwin White, *Roman Society and Roman Law in the New Testament* (Oxford: Clarendon, 1963), 188-91.

who preach, teach, and record their accounts in the generation of the eyewitnesses attest to the miracles of Christ.

Second, not all religions have reliable manuscript evidence. The New Testament has thousands of ancient manuscripts. There over five thousand Greek manuscripts, some of which are dated as early as the second century AD. If we include the early translations, we have over twenty-four thousand manuscripts. There are also quotes from the Church Fathers that date to the late first and early second century. Finally, non-Christian works, such as the writings of Thallus, Tacitus, Josephus, and others mentioned in chapter 6, corroborate several events of the life of Christ as recorded in the Gospels. The evidence shows that the eyewitness accounts were accurately preserved.

Hume's Argument Regarding the Absence of Credible Witnesses

Hume says, "There is not to be found, in all history, any miracle attested by a sufficient number of men of such unquestioned good-sense, education, and learning as to secure us against all delusion in themselves." Nor are there enough witnesses of "such undoubted integrity, as to place them beyond all suspicion of any design to deceive others." Neither are they "of such credit and reputation in the eyes of mankind, as to have a great deal to lose in case of their being detected in any falsehood."[14]

Hume's third argument is that there in fact have never been a sufficient number of educated men to "secure against delusion" and none with enough integrity to show no deception. The proven tendency of men is to readily believe the miraculous, and the many actual forgeries of miracle accounts further argue against miracles. Also, miracles abound chiefly among the uneducated and the uncultured.

In regards to the Gospel accounts of miracles, Hume states the following. First, the people were ignorant. Second, the record comes from a long period after the event. Third, there was no corroborative or concurring testimony. Finally, they resemble fabulous accounts every people have of their origins.

---

[14] Hume quoted in Norman Geisler, *Baker Encyclopedia of Christian Apologetics.*, 459.

Several historical facts refute Hume's argument. First, Christianity had numerous educated witnesses, such as Paul, who was a Jewish scholar of the law, and Luke, who was a doctor. Second, there were numerous eyewitnesses to the miracles of Christ and the resurrection as Paul mentions in 1 Corinthians 15. Scholars date the creed which Paul recites in this chapter to within three years of the resurrection. When one examines Hume's criteria, the New Testament witnesses would pass for credible witnesses.

Third, the apostles and early disciples were men and women of integrity. Several factors uphold their character. They recorded their mistakes in their accounts, they did not profit from their message, and many died for their message.

The apostles had integrity; they taught their message, lived it, and died for it. Their account was recorded in the lifetime of the eyewitnesses; moreover, it was preached and circulated not in a distant land but in the very cities of the eyewitnesses. Finally, there are Roman and Jewish sources that corroborate many facts recorded in the Gospels. Hume's arguments do not invalidate the miracle testimony of Christianity. The testimony of miracles remains a valid line of evidence for the truth of Christianity.

Conclusion

Miracles are supernatural acts of God that interrupt the natural course of events. It is reasonable to believe in miracles because God who created the universe exists. The evidence for His existence is substantial. Since there is a God who can act in history, there can be acts of God. The record of His intervention in history has been accurately recorded in the Bible. We can believe these miracles are historical because the Bible is an accurate historical document. The Gospels in particular have been proven to be very credible. The early dating of the Gospels, the fact that we have multiple written sources, and the testimony of hostile witnesses all uphold the events recorded in the Gospels. Thus, the evidence indicates we can believe in miracles.

CHAPTER 6

See a Reliable Record

I was sitting in my high school Bible class listening to our school priest explain inaccuracies and errors in the Bible. When it came to the Gospels, I was surprised to learn that they were probably not written by eyewitnesses. In fact, they were written nearly one hundred years after the life of Christ and were filled with myths that crept in as the story was orally told and retold over and over for nearly two generations. By the time the record of Christ's life was written down, these myths were part of the oral record and believed to be true. The miracle stories of Jesus walking on water and feeding five thousand with five loaves and two fish were probably mythical in nature.

A way he illustrated this was the telephone game. In this classic party game, a message is whispered in one person's ear, who then whispers it into his neighbor's ear, who then does the same. The secret message goes around to each person in the room. When the last person recites the message he received, it is hilarious to hear what he says because by the time the message gets to him, it is extremely different from the original message. This is what I was told happened to the story of Jesus as it was passed down orally from generation to generation. Therefore, the Gospels were not a historically reliable record of the life of Jesus. In fact, there was a group of renowned scholars of the Jesus Seminar whose goal was to discover the real "historical Jesus."

I was shocked to learn that we do not have an accurate portrayal of Jesus in the Gospels. I began to realize that if Jesus was simply a good teacher and not the divine Son of God, I should not trust in Him as my Lord and Savior. The teachings I received in high school and college continue to be taught in the media, in our schools, and in the culture today.

An ABC Special hosted by Peter Jennings, "The Search for the Historical Jesus," stated, "The New Testament has four different and sometimes contradictory versions of Jesus' life ... There is no reliable evidence about who the authors actually were. It is pretty much agreed that they were not eyewitnesses. In fact the Gospels were probably written nearly forty to one hundred years after Jesus' death." Mr. Jennings went on to interview top New Testament scholars who stated that many facets of the Gospel stories were simply legendary.

Another novel, *The Da Vinci Code,* made similar assertions. In this novel, Dan Brown asserts, "The Bible is a product of man, my dear. Not of God. The Bible did not fall magically from the clouds. Man created it as a historical record of tumultuous times, and it has evolved through countless translations, additions, and revisions. History has never had a definitive version of the book".[1]. Later on, he states that the four New Testament Gospels are not the earliest record of Jesus's life. There are gospels that predate the New Testament. "These are photocopies of the Nag Hammadi and Dead Sea Scrolls ... the earliest Christian records. Troublingly, they do not match up with the gospels in the Bible." Finally, he asserts that there were numerous gospel accounts, but only the four New Testament Gospels were chosen.

> Jesus Christ was a historical figure of staggering influence, perhaps the most enigmatic and inspirational leader the world has ever seen ...Understandably, His life was recorded by thousands of followers across the land ...More than eighty gospels were considered for the New Testament, and yet only a relative few were chosen for inclusion—Matthew, Mark, Luke, and John among them.[2]

---

[1]   Dan Brown, *The Da Vinci Code* (New York: Doubleday 2003), 231.
[2]   Ibid., 231.

In other words, there are "Gospels" that predate our four New Testament Gospels and they present a very different picture of Jesus. The Jennings's special and *The Da Vinci Code* shattered or seriously shook the faith of Christians throughout the world. Are the Gospels an accurate historical record of Christ? Can we trust their message? Since the New Testament Gospels give us our understanding of Jesus, it is critical that we verify their historical reliability.

The Date of the Gospels

Critics allege that the Gospels were written perhaps a generation or two after the life of Christ and, therefore, most likely were not eyewitness accounts. Let us begin with the date of Gospels. When were they written?

Noted New Testament scholar, F. F. Bruce gives strong evidence that the New Testament was completed by 100 AD and that most writings of the New Testament works were completed twenty to forty years before this.[3] Moreover, former liberal William F. Albright wrote, "We can already say emphatically that there is no longer any solid basis for dating any book of the New Testament after about AD 80, two full generations before the date between 130 and 150 given by the more radical New Testament critics of today".[4] Elsewhere Albright says, "In my opinion, every book of the New Testament was written by a baptized Jew between the forties and the eighties of the first century (very probably sometime between about AD 50 and 75)."[5]

Radical scholar John A. T. Robinson, leader of the "Death of God" movement, wrote a book titled, *Redating the New Testament*, in which he concluded that the New Testament books were written earlier than even most conservative scholars believed. He placed Matthew at 40 to after 60 AD, Mark at about 45 to 60 AD, Luke at before 57 to after 60 AD, and John at from before 40 to after 65 AD. This would mean that one or two Gospels could have been written as

---

3   F.F. Bruce, *The New Testament Documents: Are They Reliable?* (Downers Grove, IL.: InterVarsity Press, 1983), 14.
4   William Albright quoted in Norman Geisler, *Baker Encyclopedia of Christian Apologetics* (Grand Rapids, MI: Baker Books, 1999), 15.
5   William Albright quoted in Norman Geisler, *Baker Encyclopedia of Christian Apologetics*, 529.

early as seven years after the crucifixion. This means that they were all composed within the lifetimes of eyewitnesses and contemporaries of the events. Assuming the basic integrity and reasonable accuracy of the writers, this would place the reliability of the New Testament documents beyond reasonable doubt.[6]

There is strong internal and external evidence that indicate that the Gospels are written in the first century AD. There are two lines of evidence that we will investigate: the internal and external evidence.

Internal Evidence

The internal evidence supports these early dates for several reasons. The first three Gospels record Jesus' prophecy of the fall of the Jerusalem Temple which occurred in 70 AD. Despite recording Jesus' prophecy, its fulfillment is not mentioned. It is curious that these Gospels predict this happening but do not record the fulfillment of such a significant event. The Jerusalem Temple is the most significant religious structure in the life of the Jewish people. To this day, devout Jews go to the Western or Wailing Wall and pray for the rebuilding of the Temple. Why didn't the Gospel writers record its destruction? The most plausible explanation is that the Gospels were completed before its destruction.

Here is an illustration to clarify this point. Suppose you picked up a book on the history of New York City but found the first few pages missing; thus, you did not know when it was written. Despite this, you peruse through the book through to the end, but you do not see any account of the destruction of the World Trade Towers. In fact, there are no accounts of the events following that catastrophic event, such as the speech of President Bush, the rescue work at the site, and the declaration of war on the Taliban. What would you assume? You would assume this book was completed prior to the year 2001. That is what we have in the Gospels since they do not record the destruction of the most significant structure in Israel.

Further evidence is found in the book of Acts where the Temple still plays a central role in the nation of Israel. Luke wrote his Gospel before the Book of Acts. Therefore, Acts is written before 70 AD. If

---

[6]   John Robinson quoted in Norman Geisler, *Baker Encyclopedia of Christian Apologetics*, 529.

Luke precedes Acts, we can conclude Luke is written prior to 70 AD. Most scholars agree that the Gospels of Matthew and Mark precede Luke. Therefore, these Gospels are dated even earlier. So far, the internal evidence indicates that the Gospels were written before 70 AD.

However, we have strong evidence that indicates that Acts was written before 62 AD. Colin Hemer lists several reasons we can conclude this.[7] First, as mentioned earlier, there is no mention of the fall of Jerusalem in 70 AD. Second, there is no reference to the Jewish war with Rome that began in 66 AD. Third, there is no mention of Nero's persecution in 65 AD, which was one of the most severe in history. Fourth, it was under Nero that the apostles Peter and Paul were martyred, but Luke never mentions their death in Acts. It is strange that Luke mentions the deaths of less significant figures, such as the Apostle James, the brother of John, and Stephen a deacon, but he does not mention the death of the two most prominent apostles. In fact, the Book of Acts ends on a very strange note. Paul is under house arrest, and there the book suddenly ends. The most likely explanation is that Luke finished Acts before Paul's death in 65 AD. Fifth, Luke does not record the death of James, who became the leader of the church. Josephus records his death in 62 AD.[8]

An important point to remember is that the Gospel of Luke precedes Acts. If Acts were written before 62 AD, it would be more than reasonable to conclude that the Gospel of Luke was written by 60 AD or earlier. Furthermore, most scholars agree that Matthew and Mark precede the Gospel of Luke, making the dates of Matthew and Mark even earlier.

Finally, the majority of New Testament scholars believe that Paul's epistles were written from 48–60 AD. In 1 Timothy 5:18, Paul quotes from the Gospel of Luke. This shows us that Luke's Gospel was indeed completed in Paul's lifetime. This would further move up the time of the completion of Luke's gospel along with Mark and Matthew. It is not unreasonable to conclude that the three Gospels are written prior to 60 AD.

---

[7]   Colin Hemer, *The Book of Acts in the Setting of Hellenistic History* (Winona Lake, IN.: Eisenbrauns, 2001), 376-82.

[8]   Flavius Josephus, *Antiquities,* 20.9.1.

The External Evidence

The external evidence supports a first century date as well. The documentary evidence for the New Testament far surpasses any other work of its time. We have over five thousand manuscripts, and several are dated within a few years of the author's life. Here are some key documents.

An important manuscript is the Chester Beatty Papyri. It contains most of the New Testament writings and is dated 250 AD. This indicates that the original documents were written much earlier. The individual books had to be written by the original authors and then copied and eventually assembled into this early canon. The Bodmer Papyri contains most of John and dates approximately 200 AD.

Another significant manuscript is the Rylands Papyri found in Egypt. It contains a fragment of John and dates 120 AD. From this fragment, we can conclude that the Gospel of John was completed well before 120 AD because, not only did the Gospel have to be written, it had to be hand copied and made its way down from Asia Minor to Egypt, where this fragment was discovered. Since the vast majority of scholars agree that John is the last Gospel written, we can affirm its first century date along with the other three with greater assurance. Most scholars agree John wrote his Gospel in 95 AD. Therefore, this fragment dates within twenty-five years of the author's life.

Other early fragments include Papyrus 67 which contains parts of Matthew and is dated 125 AD.[9] Papyrus 64 contains parts of Matthew and is dated 125 AD.[10] Papyrus 4 contains parts of Luke and is dated 125 AD.[11] These fragments indicate that copies of the original documents existed in the early second century. We can, therefore, safely conclude that the original documents were written within the first century AD.

Another line of evidence is the Church Fathers. The Church Fathers quote the New Testament books as the authoritative and inspired Word of God as early as the late first and early second century. First,

---

[9] Craig Evans, *Fabricating Jesus* (Downers Grove, IL.: InterVarsity Press, 2006), 26.

[10] Ibid., 26

[11] Ibid., 26.

Clement of Rome sent a letter to the Corinthian church in 90 AD and quotes from the Gospels and other portions of the New Testament. Also, Papias wrote in 110 AD that Mark wrote down Peter's words and Matthew wrote his work in the Hebrew dialect.[12] Next, Ignatius, Bishop of Antioch, writes a letter before his martyrdom in Rome in 115 AD, quoting the Gospels and other New Testament letters. Moreover, Polycarp, a disciple of John, wrote to the Philippians in 120 AD and quotes from the Gospels and New Testament letters, stating Matthew, Mark, Luke, and John as the authors. Finally, Justin Martyr (150 AD) quotes from the third chapter of John. Church fathers of early second century are familiar with the apostles' writings and quote them as inspired Scripture. In fact, in the first three hundred years, the Church Fathers quote every verse of the New Testament with the exception of eleven passages.

From the internal and external evidence, we can reasonably conclude that the Gospels are written well within the first century AD. This early dating is important for several reasons. First, if the Gospels were written prior to 70 AD, they were written in the lifetime of the eyewitnesses. Therefore, it is reasonable to conclude that the Gospel writers Matthew and John were witnesses to the events they wrote about, and Luke and Mark got their accounts from the apostles themselves.

Second, early dating of the Gospels also shows that eyewitnesses were alive when the Gospels were circulating to attest to their accuracy. If the Gospels were not an accurate historical record, the enemies of the early church would have easily discredited the testimony of the apostles. If Jesus did not do the miracles they taught and wrote about, if the tomb were not empty, their accounts would have been discredited, for there were many enemies of the early Christians who were still in power and looking for any reason to discredit the credibility of their message. If the apostles were teaching myths, their message would not have lasted very long in Jerusalem where powerful the enemies of Christ remained. In fact, the apostles often appeal to the witness of the hostile crowd pointing to their knowledge of the facts as well (Acts 2:22, 26:26).

---

[12]   Timothy Jones, *Conspiracies and the Cross* (Lake Mary, FL: Strang Publications, 2008), 22.

Third, the time is too short for legends to develop. Historians agree it takes about two generations for legendary accounts to establish themselves. William Craig states, "The writings of the Greek historian Herodotus enable us to test the rate at which a legend accumulates; the tests show that even the span of two generations is too short to allow legendary tendencies to wipe out the hard core of historical fact."[13] The reason is that the witnesses must physically die so that they would not be able to discredit the legendary account.

Historical Accuracy of the Gospels

Non-Christian Historical Works

The Gospels are not only written in the lifetime of the eyewitnesses, they are also confirmed to be historically accurate works. This is attested to by non-Christian historical works and archaeology. There are nearly a dozen Roman and Jewish sources which confirm the facts of the New Testament. In fact, we could consider these sources anti-Christian sources because they are antagonistic to Christianity in their writings. In court, when the testimony of the enemy of the defense agrees or confirms the defendant's testimony, this is one of the most powerful proofs in support of the defendant. In this case, we have hostile witnesses affirming the testimony of the Gospel writers.

The Jewish sources include first the *Talmud,* which was completed in 200 AD. There are several references to Jesus, one passage of which states:

> On the eve of Passover Jesus the Nazarene was hanged. And a herald went forth before him 40 days (heralding): Jesus the Nazarene is going forth to be stoned because he practiced sorcery and instigated and seduced Israel (to idolatry). Whoever knows anything in his defense may come and state it. But since they did not find anything in his defense, they hanged him on the eve of Passover.[14]

---

[13] William Lane Craig, *The Son Rises: Historical Evidence for the Resurrection of Jesus,* (Chicago: Moody Press, 1981), 101.

[14] *Baraitha Bab. Sanhedrin 43a,* quoted in Peter Schafer, *Jesus in the Talmud* (Princeton, NJ.: Princeton University Press, 2007), 64.

In this passage, the *Talmud* and others affirm several facts that align with the Gospels: First, Jesus was a historical figure in Israel; second, Jesus was crucified; third, the time of Jesus' death, on the eve of the Passover; fourth, Jesus performed some miraculous feats, but these are attributed to sorcery and magic; finally, Jesus was condemned for leading many into apostasy.

Another Jewish source is Josephus, who recorded the history of the Jews in the first century AD. His important work, *The Antiquities*, was written about 90–95 AD. There is a famous paragraph Josephus writes about Jesus in chapter 18 of *The Antiquities*. Parts of this passage have been in question since it appears there have been some Christian interpolations added. However, historian Dr. Schlomo Pines removed the Christian additions and wrote what is likely the original statement of Josephus:

> At this time there was a wise man who was called Jesus. His conduct was good and he was known to be virtuous. And many people from among the Jews and the other nations became his disciples. Pilate condemned him to be crucified and to die. But those who became his disciples did not abandon his discipleship. They reported that he had appeared to them three days after his crucifixion, and there he was alive; accordingly he was perhaps the Messiah, concerning whom the prophets have recounted wonders.[15]

In this brief passage, Josephus affirms the message of the Gospel. First, Jesus was a genuine historical figure. Second, He lived a noble and virtuous life. Third, He gathered many followers. Fourth, He was condemned to death by Pontius Pilate. Fifth, His disciples believed they had seen Him risen from the dead. Sixth, many believed and taught He was the Messiah.

Josephus also affirms characters mentioned in the Gospels, such as the Herods; emperors Augustus, Tiberius, and Claudius; and the High Priestly families of Caiaphas, Ananias, and Annas. He also corroborates events in the Gospels, such as Judas the Galilean's

---

[15] Dr. Schlomo Pines quoted in Gary Habermas, *The Historical Jesus* (Joplin, MO.: College Press Publishing, 1996), 193-4.

uprising in Acts 5:37 (*Antiquities* 18:1:6); the famine in Acts 11:28 during the reign of Claudius (*Antiquities* 20:2:5); the sudden death of Agrippa in Acts 12 (*Antiquities* 19:8), which agrees with Luke's outline;[16] the story of John the Baptist and his death (*Antiquities* 18:5);[17] and the death account of James the brother of Jesus (*Antiquities* 20:9:1).

Roman Historical Works

Thallus wrote a work of history of Greece from the Trojan War to his present day in 52 AD. Although his work is lost, Julius Africanus in 221 AD quotes Thallus. Regarding Jesus' crucifixion, he wrote:

> On the whole world there pressed a most fearful darkness; and the rocks were rent by an earthquake, and many places in Judea and other districts were thrown down. This darkness Thallus, in the third book of his History, calls, as appears to me without reason, an eclipse of the sun.[18]

From this work, we can conclude the following: First, Jesus was crucified as recorded in the Gospels; second, the Passion story was known in Rome by 50 AD; and third, there were surprising natural anomalies that occurred connected to Jesus's death that enemies of Christianity tried to give naturalistic explanations.

Another Roman historian was Tacitus, a first century Roman historian. He recorded Nero's persecution of the Christians. In his work the *Annals*, he wrote:

> Nero fastened the guilt and inflicted the most exquisite tortures on a class hated for their abominations called Christians by the populace. Christus, from whom the name has its origin, suffered the extreme penalty during the reign of Tiberius at the hands of the procurators, Pontius Pilate, and a most mischievous superstition, thus checked for

---

16 F. F. Bruce, 105.
17 Ibid., 106–107.
18 Habermas, 197.

the moment, again broke out not only in Judea, the first source of evil, but even in Rome.[19]

Tacitus corroborates several facts of the Gospels. First, Christ was crucified. Second, he confirms the time of Christ's crucifixion as occurring during the reign of Tiberius. Third, he affirms that Pontius Pilate oversaw the death sentence of Jesus. And fourth, Christianity spread very quickly throughout the Roman Empire.

Pliny the Younger was the governor of Bithynia. During his reign, he saw that Christians were hurting the religious industry of his area and sought a way to deal with them.[20] In his tenth book, which was written about 112 AD, he wrote these words to Emperor Trajan:

> They (Christians) were in the habit of meeting on a certain fixed day before it was light, when they sang an anthem to Christ as to a god, and bound themselves by a solemn oath, not to any wicked deeds, but never to commit any fraud, theft or adultery, never to falsify their word, nor deny a trust when they should be called upon to deliver it up; after which it was their custom to separate, and then reassemble to partake of food—but of an ordinary and innocent kind.[21]

From this text, Pliny affirms three facts in this passage. First, Christians worshipped Christ as a deity from the beginning. Thus, worshipping Christ as a divine being was not invented at the Council of Nicea (325 AD) as some skeptics allege. Second, the Christians sought to reflect the moral character of Jesus. And third, communion was practiced from the beginning of the church.

Another Roman historical source comes from second century Roman philosopher Celsus. In his work, *The True Doctrine*, written in 177 AD, Celsus criticized the Christians, who claimed to be monotheists but were worshipping a man as God:

---

[19] Ibid., 188.
[20] Ed Komoszewski, James Sawyer, and Dan Wallace, *Reinventing Jesus* (Grand Rapids, MI.: Kregel Publications, 2006), 198.
[21] Habermas, 199.

Now if the Christians worshipped only one God they might have reason on their side. But as a matter of fact they worship a man who appeared only recently. They do not consider what they are doing a breach of monotheism; rather they think it perfectly consistent to worship the great God and to worship his servant as God. And their worship of this Jesus is the more outrageous because they refuse to listen to any talk about God, the father of all, unless it includes some reference to Jesus ...[22]

In this text, Celsus points out what he believes to be a clear contradiction in Christian teaching. He affirms that Christians worshipped Jesus as God and venerated Jesus with equal passion as they did for God the Father.

There are nearly a dozen Jewish and Roman historical sources that refer to Jesus. The facts mentioned in these various texts affirm the facts presented in the Gospels; we do not find them presenting facts that significantly contradict the account of Jesus's life and ministry as presented in the Gospels. Not only do we have non-Christian historical records that confirm the facts of the Gospels, there are also numerous archaeological discoveries that have validated the historical accuracy of the Gospels.

Archaeology and the Gospels

The Gospels have been confirmed by archaeology to be a very accurate historical work. Scores of discoveries have been made verifying characters, cities, events, and artifacts mentioned in the Gospels. Much more extensive treatments of this subject can be found in archaeology books. Thus, in this section, I will just touch on a few significant discoveries.

Luke, the author of the Gospel of Luke and the book of Acts, is confirmed to be a very accurate historian. One of the greatest classical archaeologists, Sir William Ramsey, a professor at Oxford and

---

[22] Celsus, *On the True Doctrine: A Discourse Against the Christians*, trans. R. Joseph Hoffman (Oxford: Oxford University Press, 1987), 116, quoted in Ed Komoszewski, James Sawyer, and Dan Wallace, *Reinventing Jesus* (Grand Rapids, MI.: Kregel Publications, 2006), 313.

Aberdeen, traveled to the Asia Minor and Palestine in an attempt to discredit Luke's work. After years of research, he concluded that Luke was a very accurate historian, and his accounts are trustworthy. He stated, "Luke's history is unsurpassed in respect of its trustworthiness."[23] He later wrote, "This author, Luke, should be placed along with the very greatest of historians."[24] Through his research, he showed that Luke accurately identified thirty-two countries, fifty-four cities, and nine islands.[25]

Luke's attention to detail and accuracy is demonstrated clearly in his titles he designates to public officials. Luke refers to government officials using the titles of proconsul, tetrach, etc. Although some are unusual, they were confirmed to be accurate. In Luke's announcement of Jesus's public ministry (Luke 3:1), he mentions, "Lysanius, tetrarch of Abilene." Scholars questioned Luke's credibility since the only Lysanius known for centuries was a ruler of Chalcis, who ruled from 40–36 BC. However, an inscription dating during the reign of Tiberius (14–37 AD) was found that names Lysanius as the "tetrarch of Abila" near Damascus.[26] This matches well with Luke's account.

Modern mariners have confirmed the accuracy of the details surrounding Paul's final journey from Palestine to Italy.[27] In Acts 17:6, Luke uses the term "politarchs" in reference to officials in Thessalonica. Skeptics thought Luke was mistaken when using this strange title. However, since the nineteenth century, numerous inscriptions have been found in Thessalonica where officials are identified as "politarchs," thus confirming Luke's accuracy.[28]

New Testament scholar F. F. Bruce wrote regarding Luke's accuracy:

---

[23] Tim LaHaye, *Jesus Who is He?* (Sisters, OR.: Multnomah Books, 1996), 49.
[24] Ibid., 48.
[25] Norman Geisler and T.A. Howe, *When Critics Ask: A Popular Handbook on Bible Difficulties* (Wheaton, IL.: Victor Books, 1992). 385.
[26] John McCray, *Archaeology and the New Testament* (Grand Rapids, MI.: Baker Books, 1996), 160.
[27] Bruce, 88.
[28] McCray, 295.

A man whose accuracy can be demonstrated in matters where we are able to test it is likely to be accurate even where the means for testing him are not available. Accuracy is a habit of mind, and we know from happy experience that some people are habitually accurate just as others can be depended upon to be inaccurate. Luke's record entitles him to be regarded as a writer of habitual accuracy.[29]

Pontius Pilate is the governor who presided over the trial of Jesus. Pilate's official residence was the coastal city of Caesarea Maritima. In 1961, a stone plaque was discovered at Caesarea's Roman Theater. Inscribed on the plaque in Latin were the words, "Pontius Pilatus, Prefect of Judea, has dedicated to the people of Caesarea a temple in honor of Tiberius." This temple is dedicated to the Emperor Tiberius who reigned from 14–37 AD. This fits well chronologically with the New Testament, which records that Pilate ruled as procurator from 26–36 AD.[30] Tacitus, a Roman historian of the first century, also confirms the New Testament designation of Pilate. He writes, "Christus, from whom the name had its origin, suffered the extreme penalty during the reign of Tiberius at the hands of one of our procurators, Pontius Pilatus."

Caiaphas was the chief priest who sentenced Jesus to death (Matthew 26). In 1990, workers digging south of the Temple Mount uncovered a burial chamber with twelve ossuaries. One was beautifully decorated and obviously belonged to a wealthy and important person. Inscribed on the ossuary was, "Caiaphas, Joseph, Son of Caiaphas." Archaeologists studied the limestone ossuary and confirmed it contained the remains of Caiaphas.[31]

For many years, skeptics questioned the crucifixion account of Jesus for no evidence of a crucified victim had ever been found. Then in 1968, a first century ossuary revealed the remains of a man who was crucified as described in the Gospels. The man's name, Yohanan ben Ha'galgol, was inscribed on the ossuary. When archaeologists studied

---

[29]   Bruce, 31.
[30]   Randal Price, *The Stones Cry Out* (Eugene, OR.: Harvest House Publishers, 1997), 307–8.
[31]   Price, 305.

the remains, they discovered he was about thirty years old. What was significant is that a seven-inch nail was found still lodged in his ankle bone![32]

Relating to the crucifixion, in 1878, a stone slab was found in Nazareth with a decree from Emperor Claudius who reigned from 41–54 AD. It stated that graves must not be disturbed nor bodies be removed. The punishment on other decrees was a fine, but this one threatened death and was dated very close to the time of the resurrection. This was probably due to Claudius investigating the riots of 49 AD. He had certainly heard of the resurrection and did not want any similar incidents. This decree was probably made in connection with the apostles' preaching of Jesus's resurrection and the Jewish argument that the body had been stolen (Matthew 28).[33]

John's accuracy has also been attested to by recent discoveries. In John 5:1–15, Jesus heals a man at the Pool of Bethesda. John describes the pool as having five porticoes. This site had long been in dispute until recently. Archaeologists discovered a pool forty feet underground with five porticoes, and the description of the surrounding area matches John's description.[34] In John 9:7, John mentions another long disputed site, the Pool of Siloam. However, this pool was also discovered in 1897, upholding the accuracy of John.[35]

This is just a brief list of discoveries that uphold the historical accuracy of the Gospels. As the years go by, new archaeological discoveries continue to confirm cities, characters, and events mentioned in the Gospels.

Are the Gospels Accurately Preserved?

Have the Gospels been accurately preserved and transmitted, or have they been edited and changed over the years? The way to test how accurate our current New Testament is to the original text depends on the amount of manuscripts available and the date of those manuscripts. The more ancient manuscripts there are, the more easily a textual scholar

---

[32] Ibid., 308–9.
[33] Norman, Geisler, *Baker Encyclopedia of Christian Apologetics*, 48.
[34] McCray, 186–8.
[35] Ibid., 188–90.

can compare the documents to see if there are errors. The closer to the date of the original author, the more accurate the work tends to be. Here is an example I use with my students to illustrate this point. Suppose I asked Jean to copy my notes. Jean, being a careful recorder, would produce an accurate copy, but we would not be surprised if she had a few minor errors. Instead, suppose I ask thirty students in class to copy my notes, and then compare their notes with one another to produce a final copy. Which of the two scenarios would yield a more accurate copy of my notes? Obviously the latter one because there are more sets of notes to compare against one another. Errors can be easily detected with more copies.

When it comes to the New Testament, how many ancient manuscripts do we have? Today we have nearly fifty-seven hundred ancient manuscripts from Europe, Africa, and the Middle East. Not only do we have ancient manuscripts, we also have the writings of the Church Fathers. As previously mentioned, in the first four hundred years of writings, the Church Fathers quote every verse in the New Testament except for eleven (mostly from 2 and 3 John). If you add the ancient translations, such as Syriac, Coptic, Latin, etc., there are nearly twenty-four thousand documents.

Now let us look at the time gap between the date of our earliest manuscripts and the author's life. One of the earliest manuscripts is the Rylands Papyri dating about 120 AD. This is a fragment of the Book of John, which was written in 95 AD.

The time gap between the original writing and the oldest manuscript of the New Testament is twenty-five years. With this small passage of time and the numerous manuscripts available, we can be assured that we have a copy that is accurate to the originals. Furthermore, texts can be compared for accuracy, and any changes or incorrect edits can be studied against the other manuscripts.

Comparing the New Testament to other works of its time reveals that the manuscript evidence for the New Testament exceeds all other historical works of its time. Here are a few examples. The writings of Plato include only seven ancient manuscripts with the earliest dating thirteen hundred years after the date of the original text. There are ten copies of the *Gallic Wars* with the earliest dating one thousand years after the original writings. *The Iliad* by Homer contain merely 643 copies. From this we see that the New Testament manuscript evidence far exceeds other works of its time. Either we must accept the accuracy of the New Testament or we must label what we know of the Greek and Roman Empire as fiction. Numerous New Testament scholars, including Westcott and Hort, Ezra Abbot, Philip Schaff, A. T. Robertson, and Bruce Metzger, write that the New Testament copy we have is 99 percent accurate to the original text.[36]

Finally, were the authors writers of integrity? First, the time period from the occurrence of events to the time of writing proves too short for legends to develop. Furthermore, they were written during the lifetimes of eyewitnesses who could either corroborate or dispute the facts. Third, the gospels do not appear to be written in the typical style of legends. They include many detailed facts that could easily be substantiated by eyewitnesses. Furthermore, they often appeal to eyewitnesses for confirmation. Luke 3:1–3 includes a detailed account regarding the time of John the Baptist's ministry. John 19 includes details of Jesus' burial place. The apostles also leave in stories that show them to be hard of heart, insensitive, cowardly, and slow to learn. These facts would likely be edited out in a legendary document. The apostles' writings also retain difficult teachings of Jesus, such as His dictates to pray for your enemies and His warnings of persecution; these are details that an editor could easily have removed. There are also specifics that illuminate the fact that the Gospels were written from four different perspectives. The differing perspectives reveal that the writers did not try to harmonize their works with one another. Finally, the apostles had nothing to gain from their message but a life of suffering and death. None of the authors renounced their faith even in the face of death. All these facts confirm that the authors of the Gospels were men of integrity writing from convictions of what they knew to be true.

---

[36] Norman Geisler, & William Nix, *A General Introduction to the Bible.* (Chicago: Moody Press 1986), 474.

Are There Missing Gospels?

There are some scholars who allege that there are secret Gospels that were excluded from the New Testament in an effort to preserve a false image of Jesus—that He was the divine Son of God—which developed in the fourth century AD. According to proponents of this view, the earliest accounts of Jesus are found amongst the Dead Sea Scrolls and the Gnostic gospels found in Nag Hammadi, Egypt. This theory was made popular by the bestselling novel, *The Da Vinci Code,* in which author Dan Brown claims there were eighty gospels, but only four were chosen to be part of the New Testament. Here are two excerpts from this novel:

> Jesus Christ was a historical figure of staggering influence, perhaps the most enigmatic and inspirational leader the world has ever seen … Understandably, His life was recorded by thousands of followers across the land … More than eighty gospels were considered for the New Testament and yet only a relative few were chosen for inclusion—Matthew, Mark, Luke, and John among them.[37]

> "Fortunately for historians," Teabing said, "some of the gospels that Constantine attempted to eradicate managed to survive. The Dead Sea Scrolls were found in the 1950s hidden in a cave near Qumran in the Judean desert. And of course the Coptic Scrolls in 1945 at Nag Hammadi … these documents speak of Christ's ministry in very human terms. Of course, the Vatican, in keeping with their tradition of misinformation, tried very hard to suppress the release of these scrolls. And why wouldn't they? The scrolls highlight glaring historical discrepancies and fabrications, clearly confirming that the modern Bible was compiled and edited by men who possessed a political agenda—to promote the divinity of the man Jesus Christ and use His influence to solidify their own power base."[38]

Brown's assertions are similar to those presented by the Jesus Seminar, a gathering of liberal theologians who have concluded that 80 percent of what is now written in our Gospels is not part of the

---

[37] Brown, 231.
[38] Brown, 234.

original New Testament text. Jesus Seminar leader John Dominic Crossan writes, "Those four gospels do not represent all the early gospels available or even a random sample within them, but are instead a calculated collection known as the canonical gospels. This becomes clear in studying other gospels either discerned as sources inside the official four or else discovered as documents outside them."[39] Are the secret gospels at Nag Hammadi and the Dead Sea the earliest record of Christ? Let us begin by looking at the Dead Sea Scrolls.

The Dead Sea Scrolls, which were discovered in 1948, contained the ancient writings of the Essenes, a monastic group that lived in the Dead Sea region. They viewed the religious culture of Israel to be corrupt and chose to separate themselves from society and spend their days studying and copying the Old Testament. The Dead Sea Scrolls contained the rules and regulations of Essene life, but fragments from all the Old Testament books, except for Esther, were also found among the scrolls. No New Testament documents were found in this collection of manuscripts.

The Dead Sea Scrolls provided valuable bibliographic evidence and demonstrated that our present day Old Testament is accurately preserved. However, the Dead Sea Scrolls in no way provide proof that any secret gospels exist. Instead, they confirm the accurate preservation of the Old Testament text and the prophetic nature of the Messianic prophecies of Christ.

The Nag Hammadi Texts, discovered in 1946, are named after the place they were found on the west bank of the Nile. A library was found containing forty-five texts written in the Coptic language. These were written from the early second century to the fourth century AD. Examples of texts included *The Gospel of Thomas, The Gospel of Philip, The Acts of Peter,* and others. These texts were Gnostic in character and found in a library of Gnostic works. Prior to this discovery, our knowledge of the Gnostics had only come from the criticisms of the Church Fathers of the Gnostic texts, but now we can read the Gnostics for what they actually say.

---

[39]   John Dominic Crossan, *Jesus A Revolutionary Biography,* (San Francisco, CA.: Harper Collins Publishers, 1989), X.

Gnosticism derives its meaning from the Greek word *gnosis,* which means "knowledge." Gnosticism taught the secret knowledge of dualism: that the material world was evil and the spiritual realm was pure. Since the physical realm is evil, they taught that Jesus was not really human, and He did not really die on a cross. They further taught that Jesus shared secret knowledge with a select few, and that only those with keen insight into these secrets could truly release the divine within them.

Contrary to the assertion of the novel, these gospels were never secret; we have known of them for centuries. The early Church Fathers wrote about the texts and rejected them as uninspired and nonapostolic. For example, Iraneaus (130–200 AD) and Tertullian (160–225 AD) mentioned the texts in their letters and stated their rejection of them. These texts were never considered part of the inspired writing of the apostles for several reasons.

First, many of the texts are dated well after the death of the apostles. Also, the teachings are inconsistent with previous revelations of Jesus and apostolic teaching. The teaching of Gnostic dualism is what the Gospels of John and his epistles appear to be reacting against. Additionally, the Church Fathers knew of these texts and never regarded them as equal to the Gospels. The secret teachings for a select few go against the nature of the Gospel. Christ taught His followers to go and preach the teachings of Christ throughout the world in an honest and open manner.

Furthermore, the Gnostics rejected orthodox Christianity, and orthodox Christianity rejected the Gnostics. The two teachings were not compatible in any way. The four Gospels were known to be apostolic writings, but these others texts were not. A brief reading of these Gnostic works reveal they are very different in nature from the New Testament. Following are some excerpts from several Gnostic texts.

From the *Gospel of Philip*, a second century AD document, we read this passage:

> Light and Darkness, life and death, right and left, are brothers of one another. They are inseparable. Because of this neither are the good good, nor evil evil, nor is life life, nor death death. For this reason each one will dissolve into its earliest origin. But those who are exalted above the world are indissoluble, eternal.

The above passage teaches that good and evil, life and death, light and darkness exist in a harmonious relationship; however, this contradicts biblical teachings. John 1:5 states, "In him was life and that life was the light of men. The light shines in the darkness, but the darkness has not overcome it". Moreover, John 8:12 states, "Again Jesus spoke to them saying, 'I am the light of the world. Whoever follows me will not walk in darkness, but will have the light of life' ". Finally, 1 John 1:5 makes it very clear that there is indeed a stark contrast between light and darkness: "God is light and in Him is no darkness at all".

Passages from John's writings teach that life and death, God and sin, light and darkness live in opposition to one another, and one will overcome the other. There will not be a harmonious symbiotic relationship, but rather a conflict in which God, who is light, life, and goodness, will triumph.

Another passage from the *Gospel of Philip* states:

> This is quite in keeping with the truth. But you saw something of that place, and you became those things. You saw the Spirit, you became spirit. You saw Christ, you became Christ. You saw the Father, you shall become Father. So in this place you see everything and do not see yourself, but in that place you do see yourself—and what you see you shall become.

The above passage also contradicts biblical teaching. Believers reflect the character of Christ, but will never become God or Christ. God remains sovereign over all His creation. Believers are taught to be holy but not divine in nature.

The *Gospel of Mary Magdalene*, a third century work, produces some deviant teaching as well. Verses 25–26 states: "Peter said to him, 'Since you have explained everything to us, tell us this also: What is the sin of the world?' The Savior said, 'There is no sin, but it is you who make sin when you do the things that are like the nature of adultery, which is called sin.'"

Central to biblical Christianity is that we are all guilty of sin and in need of the saving work of Christ upon the cross (Romans 3:23 and 1 John 1:8–9). It would be completely inconsistent for Christ to teach that He had to die for the sins of mankind when sin was not a reality but a state of mind.

Chapter 10:39–42 from the *Gospel of Peter*, dating from the second century AD, presents a story that would appear to be more mythical than historical. It states that the tomb of Christ was:

Opened and both of the young men entered in. When therefore those soldiers saw that, they waked up the centurion and the elders (for they also were there keeping watch); and while they were yet telling them the things which they had seen, they saw again three men come out of the sepulchre, and two of them sustaining the other (lit. the one), and a cross following, after them. And of the two they saw that their heads reached unto heaven, but of him that was led by them that it over passed the heavens. And they heard a voice out of the heavens saying: Hast thou (or Thou hast) preached unto them that sleep? And an answer was heard from the cross, saying: Yea.

In the above passage there is a walking and talking cross. Along with that, the necks of the angels stretch far up into the heavens. In contrast to this passage, within the Gospels, there are miracle accounts that are supernatural but not strange. This passage presents a story that is both strange and mythical in character.

Finally, from the *Gospel of Thomas*, verse 114, a second century work, appears the following passage:

Simon Peter said to them, "Make Mary leave us, for females don't deserve life." Jesus said, "Look, I will guide her to make her male, so that she too may become a living spirit resembling you males. For every female who makes herself male will enter the kingdom of Heaven."

Scripture teaches that we are created in God's image, male and female (Genesis 1:27). First Peter 3:7 states, "Likewise, husbands, live with your wives in an understanding way, showing honor to the woman as the weaker vessel, since they are heirs with you of the grace of life, so that your prayers may not be hindered". The Bible teaches that women are also created in the image of God and are heirs to eternal life. Never do we find in Scripture that women are unworthy of salvation and that they need to transform their gender to inherit eternal life.

The theory that there exist secret gospels that predate the New Testament is false. First, there are no New Testament documents amongst the Dead Sea Scrolls. Second, the Gnostic texts from Nag Hammadi are not a secret and were never covertly suppressed by the early church. The Church Fathers knew of these writings, rejected them from the very beginning, and never considered them to be apostolic. Also, the Gnostic teachings within them make them inconsistent with previous revelations. The apostles in their writings, especially John, reject Gnostic teaching. Finally, the unorthodox theology and stories within these texts leads one to conclude these are neither inspired nor apostolic in origin. Therefore, the claim that there are secret gospels is fiction.

Conclusion

The evidence reveals that the Gospels are an accurate historical work written by first century eyewitnesses or their close associates (Mark and Luke). Their early dates are confirmed by the internal and external evidence. Moreover, their historical accuracy is confirmed by both non-Christian historical works and archaeology. The manuscript evidence demonstrates that the Gospels have been accurately preserved and have not been significantly altered. We can then reasonably conclude that the Gospels give us an accurate historical account of the life of Jesus, who claimed to be the divine Son of God and confirmed His claims through His miraculous, sinless life, death, and resurrection.

CHAPTER 7

See a Unique Savior

I was speaking at a university in Dallas before an audience of mainly foreign graduate students. As I began to speak, a man named Michael came up to the podium and interrupted me as part of a plan about which the audience was unaware. He informed us that he had an important message he needed to share. I allowed him to speak to the audience. Looking straight at the audience, he announced, "I was meditating this afternoon, and my higher self revealed to me this truth that I am God. So I am here today to let you know I love you, and I am here to receive your praise and worship tonight."

Immediately, the audience began to "boo" him and even throw wads of paper at him. I stepped up, silenced the crowd, and asked, "Why are you booing this man? Why don't you believe what he is saying?" Immediately, one man stood and said, "Alright, if you are God, turn water into wine!" Another man stood up and shouted, "Why don't you walk on water for us?" To these taunts, Michael responded, "Don't challenge me. Just trust what I say, and you will be filled with joy." After several minutes of questioning and jeering from the crowd, I stepped up and asked the audience, "Is this man a good and wise teacher?" The audience responded, shouting, "He is insane!" "Put him in a mental hospital!" I again asked, "Why don't you consider him a great teacher?" Several grad students shouted, "Because anyone who thinks they are God is clearly insane and cannot be a good teacher!"

I then looked at the audience and stated, "These are the same kinds of claims Jesus made about Himself. If you think Michael is insane, what about Jesus who claimed to be God in the flesh?" There was complete silence in the room. I stated, "You must make your decision today. Either Jesus was an insane madman, the devil from hell, or was indeed the divine Son of God. There is no other choice. A man who made these kinds of claims cannot be considered simply a good teacher." After a moment of silence, I began my presentation by saying, "Either Jesus was a liar, a lunatic, or He really was the Lord of all creation." Throughout the presentation, I had their attention.

The Astounding Claims of Jesus

We established in the previous chapter that the Gospels are an accurate historical account of the life and ministry of Jesus. Jesus made some outrageous claims that no ordinary person would dare to make. First, He claimed to be God. His statements of equality with God meant that He believed that He possessed the authority and attributes of God and was willing to receive the adoration belonging to God. He proclaimed authority over creation, forgiveness of sins, and life and death. He declared to possess the attributes of God. He emphatically stated that He was the source of truth and the only way to eternal life. Among the significant leaders of history, only Jesus made such claims.

There are a variety of outrageous claims made by Jesus. In John 14:8–9, Philip made a specific request to Jesus. "Philip said to him, 'Lord, show us the Father, and it is enough for us.' Jesus said to him, 'Have I been with you so long, and you still do not know me, Philip? Whoever has seen me has seen the Father.'" We also read in John 10:30 that when the Pharisees disparaged Jesus and challenged Him, He responded, "I and the Father are one." The text continues: "The Jews picked up stones again to stone him. Jesus answered them, 'I have shown you many good works from the Father; for which of them are you going to stone me?' The Jews answered him, 'It is not for a good work that we are going to stone you but for blasphemy, because you, being a man, make yourself God'" (John 10:31–33). It is clear in these two statements, Jesus claimed to be God. His opponents clearly understood His declaration of equality with God.

When scholars challenged Him regarding His authority over Abraham, the father of the Jews, Jesus replied, "Your father Abraham rejoiced that he would see my day. He saw it and was glad." So the Jews said to him, "You are not yet fifty years old, and have you seen Abraham?" Jesus said to them, "Truly, truly, I say to you, before Abraham was, I am" (John 8:56–58). Jesus clearly claimed to have existed two thousand years earlier and to have known Abraham. Moreover, His use of the statement, "I am," is an obvious reference to God's revelation of His name to Moses in Exodus 3:14. The audience to whom Jesus spoke clearly understood this, hence their desire to stone Him for blasphemy.

On the issue of life and death Jesus stated, "I am the resurrection and the life. Whoever believes in me, though he die, yet shall he live" (John 11:25). Here, He states His authority over life and death. The Jews understood that this authority was reserved for God, the source of life.

Finally, Jesus accepted and encouraged others to worship Him. Throughout the Gospels, the disciples worshipped Jesus, as seen in Matthew 14:33 and John 9:38. Jesus stated in John 5:22–23, "The Father judges no one, but has given all judgment to the Son, that all may honor the Son, just as they honor the Father. Whoever does not honor the Son does not honor the Father who sent him." Jesus knew the Old Testament command "You shall worship the Lord your God, and him only shall you serve" (Matthew 4:10). Despite this, Jesus encouraged others to worship Him. Either He was mad, or He was who He claimed to be and deserves our worship as God incarnate.

After reading such claims, it is impossible for anyone to say He was merely a good teacher. A man making claims like these must either be a diabolical liar, insane, or truly God incarnate. C. S. Lewis wrote:

> I am trying here to prevent anyone saying the really foolish thing that people often say about Him: "I'm ready to accept Jesus as a great moral teacher, but I don't accept His claim to be God." That is the one thing we must not say. A man who was merely a man and said the sort of things Jesus said would not be a great moral teacher. He would either be a lunatic—on a level with the man who says he is a poached egg—or else he would be the Devil of Hell. You

must make your choice. Either this man was, and is, the Son of God: or else a madman or something worse. You can shut Him up for a fool, you can spit at Him and kill Him as a demon; or you can fall at His feet and call Him Lord and God. But let us not come with any patronizing nonsense about Him being a great human teacher. He has not left that open to us. He did not intend to.[1]

The claims of Christ make Him unique from all other major religious leaders. Muhammad claimed to be the prophet of God. Buddha claimed to be the one who showed the way. Confucius was a teacher who taught the principles that would make for an ideal society. Jesus made the unique and astonishing claim to be the divine Son of God. It is time to examine which of these conclusions is most plausible.

Liar, Lunatic, Legend, or Lord?

We have established at this point that Jesus made some astounding claims about Himself. He presumed to be God, claimed the authority and attributes of God, and encouraged others to worship Him as God. If, however, Jesus was a liar, He knew His message was false and was willing to deceive thousands with claims He knew were untrue. That is, Jesus knew that He was not God, He did not know the way to eternal life, and He died and sent thousands to their deaths for a message He knew was a lie. This would make Jesus history's greatest villain (and perhaps a demon) for teaching this wicked lie. He would have also been history's greatest fool, for it was these claims that lead Him to His death.

Few, if any, seriously hold to this position. Even the skeptics unanimously agree that He was at least a great moral teacher. William Lecky, one of Britain's most respected historians and an opponent of Christianity writes, "It was reserved for Christianity to present the world an ideal character, which through all the changes of eighteen centuries has inspired the hearts of men with an impassioned love."[2]

---

[1]   C. S. Lewis, *Mere Christianity* (New York: Macmillan Publishing, 1960), 55-6.

[2]   William Lecky, *History of European Morals from Augustus to Charlemagne* (New York: D. Appleton and Company, 1903), 8 quoted in Josh McDowell, *The New Evidence That Demands a Verdict* (Nashville: Thomas Nelson Publishers, 1999), 159.

However, it would be inconsistent and illogical to believe that Jesus was a great moral teacher if some of those teachings contained immoral lies about Himself. He would have to be a stupendous hypocrite to teach others honesty and virtue and while preaching the lie that He was God. It is inconceivable to think that such deceitful, selfish, and depraved acts could have issued forth from the same one who otherwise maintained from beginning to end the purest and noblest character known in history.

Since the liar conclusion is not logical, let us assume He really believed He was God but was mistaken. If He truly believed He had created the world, had seen Abraham two thousand years before, and had authority over death, and yet none of this was true, we can only conclude that He was insane.

However, when one studies the life of Jesus, He clearly does not display the characteristics of insanity. The abnormality and imbalance we find in a deranged person are not there. His teachings, such as the Sermon on the Mount, remain some of the greatest ever recorded. Jesus was continually challenged by the Pharisees and lawyers, highly educated men whose modern day equivalent would be our university professors. They were fluent in several languages and were known for their scholarship of the Old Testament and Jewish law. They challenged Jesus with some of the most profound questions of their day, and Jesus' quick answers amazed and silenced them. In the face of tremendous pressure, we find He exemplified the greatest composure. For these reasons, the lunatic argument is not consistent.

The third option, which very few historians hold, is that Jesus was not a historical person but a mythical figure. However, as shown in the previous chapter, there is too much historical evidence against this option. The New Testament is a very accurate historical record, and it affirms that Jesus was a historical figure. The New Testament was also written in the lifetime of the eyewitnesses, and it would have been impossible for the apostles to preach their message in the face of the eyewitnesses if Jesus did not exist and had not done the works they were proclaiming He did. We also have nearly a dozen non-Christian historical works that confirm Jesus as a historical figure. Due to the substantial amount of evidence, few historians entertain this possibility.

If these three—the liar, the lunatic, and the legend—are not consistent with the facts, we must take a serious look at the fourth option: that Jesus was really who He said He was—God incarnate. The next question is whether He proved to have the credentials of God? Let's investigate this possibility.

Is He Lord?

Thus far, we have learned that Jesus is unique among all men for the profound statements He made about His divinity. We concluded that it is impossible to state He was simply a good, moral teacher. From His amazing statements, He must be a liar, a lunatic, a legend, or God. Since the first three were not conceivable, we will begin looking at the fourth alternative: that He really is God.

First, we must see if He confirmed His claims. In Chapter Three, we learned that God confirms His message and His messengers with miracles. Jesus confirmed His claim through miraculous confirmation. No one demonstrated authority over every realm of creation as Jesus did. He is unique in His miraculous confirmations of His claim.

Confirmation of Miracles

If a person claimed to be God, we would expect Him to do the supernatural. We would expect Him to demonstrate authority over every realm of creation, such as nature, sickness, sin, and death. Jesus demonstrated such authority. Jesus' miracles demonstrated His power over creation, sickness, and death. He demonstrated His authority over nature in such miracles as walking on water (Matthew 14:25), multiplying bread (Matthew 14:15–21), and calming the storm (Mark 4:35–41). He demonstrated authority over sickness with His healings of terminal diseases. Moreover, His healings did not take weeks or days, but were instantaneous. He healed blindness (John 9), paralysis (Mark 2), leprosy (Luke 17), and deafness (Mark 7). Such miracles cannot be attributed to psychosomatic healing, but to the One who rules over creation.

No other individual demonstrated such authority. Muhammad does not confirm his prophetic claim with miracles. He is asked in the *Quran* to present miraculous confirmation of his prophetic call, but he refuses to do so. He simply tells people to look at the *Quran*, and that should suffice (Surah 3:181–4 and 28:47–53). He does not demonstrate authority over creation as Jesus did. However, the *Quran* does affirm that Jesus did miracles (Sura 3:37–45 and 5:110). The miracle accounts of Muhammad appear in the *Hadith,* which was written nearly two hundred years after Muhammad's life. Buddha does not perform any miracles. Miracle accounts of Buddha do not appear till centuries later. When it comes to Christ, we have first-generation historical accounts of His life. The miracles Jesus performed set Him apart from any individual who ever lived.

Some people doubt whether these miracles occurred, viewing the miracle accounts as fictitious legends developed after the death of Christ. Philosopher David Hume argued that human nature tends to gossip and exaggerate the truth. Others argue that the miracle accounts were propagated in distant lands by the followers of Christ well after the events so that the miracle accounts could not have been verified due to distance and time.

However, as demonstrated in the previous chapter, the New Testament has proven to be a historically reliable document. Second, also as demonstrated in the previous chapter, there is strong evidence that supports the conclusion that the Gospels were written within the first century AD. Numerous ancient manuscripts confirm a first century dating of the Gospels as well as their accurate recording and transmission. Along with these ancient manuscripts are the writings of the Church Fathers, who quote the Gospels as early as the late first century and early second century AD.

It is true that legends develop when followers travel to distant lands well after the time of the events and tell of stories which cannot be confirmed. However, legends usually develop at least two generations after the death of the eyewitnesses, at which time it is very difficult to verify any of the accounts since all available witnesses are not available. However, the miracle accounts of Jesus were being told in the very cities in which they occurred during the lifetime of those who witnessed the events. Those who witnessed the miracles were both followers of Christ and His enemies. These eyewitnesses were questioned carefully by those in authority. If any claims were exaggerated or distorted, they could have easily been refuted. The New

Testament, with its miracle accounts, could not have survived had the accounts not been true, for there were too many eyewitnesses who could have refuted their accounts. First century eyewitnesses attest to the miracles of Jesus, and these events are recorded and circulated in the lifetime of the eyewitnesses, assuring us that the miracles of Jesus did indeed occur as recorded in the Gospels.

Prophetic Legacy

One of the most incredible types of evidence is the testimony of prophecy. The Old Testament contains a number of messianic prophecies made centuries before Christ appeared on the earth. The fact that He fulfilled each one is powerful testimony that He was no ordinary man. Allow me to illustrate this point using eight prophecies:

1. Genesis 12:1–3 states the Messiah would come from the seed of Abraham.
2. Genesis 49:10 states that He would be of the tribe of Judah.
3. Second Samuel 7:12 states that Messiah would be of the line of King David.
4. Micah 5:2 states that He would be born in the city of Bethlehem.
5. Daniel 9:24–27 states that He would die or be "cut off" exactly 483 years after the declaration to reconstruct the temple in 444 BC.
6. Isaiah 53 states that the Messiah would die with wicked men and be buried in a rich man's tomb.
7. Psalm 22:16 states that upon His death, His hands and His feet would be pierced. This is quite significant since Roman crucifixion had not been invented at the time the psalmist was writing.
8. Isaiah 49:7 states that Messiah would be known and hated by the entire nation. Not many men become known by their entire nation, and even less are despised by the entire nation.

Now calculate the possibility of someone fulfilling these by coincidence. Let us suppose there is an estimated one in one hundred chance a man could fulfill just one of these prophecies by chance. That would mean when all eight are put together, there is a $1/10^{16}$ probability that they were fulfilled by chance. Mathematician Peter Stoner estimates $1/10^{17}$ possibility that these prophecies were fulfilled by chance.[3] Mathematicians have estimated that the possibility of sixteen of these prophecies being fulfilled by chance is about $1/10^{40}$.[4] That's a decimal point followed by forty-four zeroes and a one! These figures show it is extremely improbable that these prophecies could have been fulfilled by chance. The figures for fulfillment of the 109 major prophecies are staggering.[5]

Skeptics have objected to the testimony of prophecy, stating they were written after the times of Jesus and, therefore, fulfill themselves. However, the evidence overwhelmingly shows these prophecies were clearly written centuries before Christ. Most scholars agree that the Old Testament canon was completed by 450 BC. The *Septuagint*, the Greek translation of the Old Testament, was completed in the reign of Ptolemy Philadelphus in 250 BC. The Dead Sea Scrolls, discovered in 1948, contained fragments from all the books of the Old Testament, with the exception of Esther. Books were dated as early as the third century BC. The famous scroll of Isaiah was dated by paleographers to be written in 100 BC.[6] This book alone contains numerous prophecies Christ fulfilled. The Dead Sea Scrolls confirmed the messianic prophecies were written centuries before Christ, and no religious leader has fulfilled anything close to the number of prophecies Jesus fulfilled.

Sinless

Another remarkable and unique character quality was that Jesus was sinless. Throughout His ministry, even His enemies could not level a charge against Him. In John 8, Jesus boldly proclaims His deity by announcing that Abraham rejoiced to see Him. The Jews, in anger,

---

[3]   Josh McDowell, *The New Evidence That Demands a Verdict* (Nashville, TN.:: Thomas Nelson Publishers, 1999), 193-4.

[4]   Norman Geisler, *When Skeptics Ask* (Wheaton, IL: Victor Press, 1990), 116.

[5]   Tim LaHaye, *Jesus, Who is He?* (Sisters, OR: Multnomah Books, 1996), 176.

[6]   Norman Geisler and William Nix, *A General Introduction to the Bible* (Chicago: Moody Press, 1986), 365-66.

began looking for something to accuse Him of. To their response, Jesus asked them, "Which one of you convicts me of sin?" (John 8:46). To this challenge, His enemies had no legitimate response. Certainly if there had been some sin in which they could have identified, they certainly would have done so.

During His trial, the Jewish leaders tried to level some charge against Him. Pontius Pilate, hearing their charges, in the end declared that Jesus was innocent of the charges leveled against Him (Luke 23:14).

Even Christ's closest associates declared that He was sinless. In 2 Corinthians 5:21, Paul states, "For our sake he made him to be sin who knew no sin, so that in him we might become the righteousness of God." In First Peter 2:22, Peter states, "He committed no sin; neither was deceit found in his mouth." John writes in 1 John 3:5, "You know that he appeared to take away sins, and in him there is no sin." Christ taught them to confess their sins, but of Himself, there was no need for Him to confess any sin.

No other individual in history can make the claim of being sinless. Muhammad is told to confess his sins several times in the *Quran*. Muslims claim that after his prophetic call, Muhammad did not sin; however, this claim can hardly be defended. For example, after his prophecy, Muhammad believed he received a revelation allowing Muslims to worship the three gods of the Quraysh tribe. However, he later admitted that Satan possessed him when he uttered those verses.[7] Buddhists do not claim Gautama lived a perfectly sinless life. No Hindu guru would claim to have lived a sinless life. Only Jesus lived a sinless life. This reflects the character of God who alone is holy.

Remarkable Impact on the World

The impact of Jesus upon the world is unique. He has impacted civilization in tremendous ways in the areas of medicine, science, art, literature, music, education, and government. More hospitals and schools have been started in the name of Jesus than any other person in history. There is more art, music, and literature written about and in reference

---

[7] Ibn Ishaq, *The Life of Muhammad*, trans. A. Guillaume (Karachi, Pakistan: Oxford University Press, 1955), 165-6 & *Qur'an* 22:52, 53:19-23.

to Jesus than any other person in history. More systems of justice and ethics have been built on the teachings of Jesus than any other person in history. His impact has been phenomenal, especially given that this is a man who never sat on an earthly throne, commanded a government, or wrote a bestselling piece of literature. Instead, He was born in an obscure little town, raised by humble parents, taught for only three years, and died a criminal's death.

His impact on human civilization indeed makes Him unique. An anonymous author penned these words about the astounding impact of Jesus upon our world:

> Nineteen centuries have come and gone, and today He is the central figure for much of the human race. All the armies that ever marched, and all the navies that ever sailed, and all the parliaments that ever sat, and all the kings that ever reigned, put together have not affected the life of man upon this earth as powerfully as this "One Solitary Life."[8]

The impact Jesus has made on civilization marks Him as a unique individual. His life and teachings have transformed more lives and more societies than any other individual.

Authority over Death

The miracles Jesus performed remain unequaled by anyone. One of the most impressive displays of His authority was His demonstration of authority as revealed in His power over sin and death. There are many religions and religious leaders who claim to know what lies beyond the grave. The problem is that no one has demonstrated authority over the grave or confirmed their belief of what happens after death. Only Jesus demonstrated authority over death, the undefeatable enemy.

During His three-year ministry, Jesus exercised His authority over death by raising several people from the grave (Matthew 9 and Luke 7). Most notable is the account of Lazarus found in John 11. Here, even in the face of His enemies, Jesus raised Lazarus from the grave.

---

[8] Anonymous, "One Solitary Life," quoted in Tim LaHaye, *Jesus Who is He?* (Sisters, OR.: Multnomah Books, 1996), 68.

In Hawaiian legend, there is a famous story of a mythical hero named Maui. According to Hawaiian lore, Maui captured the sun and fought supernatural beings. However, there was one enemy Maui could not defeat. One day, he saw his earthly mother aging, and he asked her how can death be defeated? She told Maui that the only way to defeat death was to enter the deep caverns of the volcano and take its heart while death lay asleep. According to the legend, Maui descended one evening into the caverns of the volcano and secretly entered into the mouth of death. However, as he began pulling its heart, a bird awakened death and killed Maui. Death has not been mastered by any individual, but Christ demonstrated authority over this foe.

Paul writes in First Corinthians 15 that Christ has defeated death. No individual demonstrates authority over life and death. Only God is capable of creating and restoring life. Jesus demonstrated His deity by displaying the authority God alone possesses.

Are Christ's Miracles Borrowed From Mystery Religions?

One of the popular ideas being promoted today, especially on the Internet, is the idea that the miracle stories of Jesus were borrowed from ancient pagan myths. Timothy Freke and Peter Gandy write in their book *The Laughing Jesus,*

> "Each mystery religion taught its own version of the myth of the dying and resurrecting Godman, who was known by different names in different places. In Egypt, where the mysteries began, he was Osiris. In Greece, he became Dionysus, in Asia Minor, he is known as Atis, in Syria, he is Adonis, in Persia, he is Mithras, in Alexandria, he is Serapis, to name a few."[9]

Proponents of this idea point out that there are several parallels between these pagan myths and the story of Jesus Christ. Parallels include a virgin birth, a divine Son of God, the god dying for mankind, and resurrection from the dead. Skeptics allege that Christianity did

---

[9]   Timothy Freke and Peter Gandy, *The Laughing Jesus* (New York: Three Rivers Press, 2005), 55-56, quoted in Lee Strobel, *The Case for the Real Jesus* (Grand Rapids, MI: Zondervan Publishing, 2007),158.

not present any unique teaching but rather borrowed the majority of their tenets from the mystery religions.

This position was taught in the nineteenth century, but by the mid-twentieth century, this view was shown to be false and abandoned even by those who believed Christianity was purely a natural religion.[10] The resurgence of this theory can be attributed to recent novels like *The Da Vinci Code* and the promotion of the idea by the "new atheists" distributing information through the Internet.

To create the illusion of parallels between the Gospels and the Greek myths, proponents of this view distort the information using the following methods. First, they combine the pagan religions, treating them as if they are one religion when making comparisons to Christianity. By combining features from various religions, an attempt is made to show strong parallels.[11] However, when the individual myths themselves are studied, the reader will soon find major differences with very little commonality.

Second, Christian terms are used to describe pagan beliefs, and then it is concluded that there are parallel origins and meanings. However, although the terms used are the same, there is a big difference between the Christian practice and definition from the pagan understanding.[12]

Third, there is an error in the chronology. Supporters of this theory incorrectly assume that Christianity borrowed many of its ideas from the mystery religions when the evidence reveals it was actually the other way around. There is no archaeological evidence that mystery religions were in Palestine in first century AD. Jews and early Christians despised the pagan religions and would avoid any syncretism with other religions. Jews and Christians were uncompromisingly monotheistic while Greeks were polytheistic. Christians also strongly defended the uniqueness of Christ as the only Son of God and the only way to eternal life (Acts 4:12). Although early Christians encountered pagan religions, they opposed any adopting of foreign beliefs.[13] Ron Nash

---

[10]   Ed Komoszewski, James Sawyer, and Daniel Wallace, *Reinventing Jesus* (Grand Rapids, MI: Kregel Publications, 2006), 221.

[11]   Ibid., 223-24.

[12]   Ibid., 224-26.

[13]   Ibid., 231-34.

stated, "The uncompromising monotheism and the exclusiveness that the early church preached and practiced make the possibility of any pagan inroads ... unlikely if not impossible."[14]

Fourth, Christianity has a linear view of history, meaning history is moving in a purposeful direction. There is a purpose for mankind's existence, and history is moving in a direction to fulfill God's plan for the ages. The mystery religions have a circular view of history. History continues in a never-ending cycle or repetition often linked with the vegetation cycle.[15]

Christianity gains its source from Judaism, not Greek mythology. Jesus, Paul, and the apostles appeal to the Old Testament, and there are direct teachings and fulfillments in the Old Testament. Teachings such as one God, blood atonement for sin, salvation by grace, sinfulness of mankind, and bodily resurrection are sourced in Judaism and foreign to Greek mythology. The idea of resurrection was not taught in any Greek mythological work prior to the late second century AD.[16]

Legends of the Mystery Religions

A brief study of the legends soon reveals that there are few, if any, alleged parallels to the life of Jesus Christ. Historians acknowledge that several variations to many of these myths exist, and that they also evolved and changed along with the Roman culture and later, Christianity influenced them. Historical research indicates that it was not until the third century AD that Christianity and the mystery religions came into real contact with one another.[17] A brief overview of some of the most popular myths reveals the lack of resemblance to Christianity.

Myth of Resurrection

There are major differences when describing a resurrection between Christianity and pagan myths. First, none of the resurrections in these myths involve the God of the universe dying a voluntary death for

---

14   Ron Nash, *Gospel and the Greeks* (Dallas: Word Books, 1992), 168.
15   Komoszewski, Sawyer, and Wallace, 221.
16   Gary Habermas, *The Historical Jesus* (Joplin, MO: College Press Publishing, 1997), 34.
17   Nash, 129.

his creation. Only Jesus died for sins; the death of other gods was due to hunting accidents, emasculation, etc. The gods die by compulsion and not by choice, sometimes in bitterness and despair, but never in self-giving love.[18]

Second, Jesus died once for all (Hebrews 7:27, 9:25–28) while pagan gods repeat the death and rebirth cycle yearly with the seasons. Third, unlike the Greek gods, Jesus died voluntarily for mankind. Fourth, Jesus's death was not a defeat, but a triumph. The New Testament's mood of victory and joy (1 Corinthians 15:50–57 and Colossians 2:13–15) stands in contrast to pagan myths, whose mood is dark and sorrowful over the fate of their gods. Finally, Jesus' death was an actual event in history. Christianity insists and defends the historical credibility of the Gospel accounts while the pagan cults make no such attempt.[19]

Two popular myths that some believe parallel the resurrection of Christ are the stories of Osiris and Attis. The cult of the god Osiris and his wife Isis originate in Egypt. According to the legend, Osiris' wicked brother Set murdered him by entrapping him in a coffin and sinking the coffin to the bottom of the Nile. Isis recovered the coffin and returned it to Egypt. However, Set discovered the body, dismembered it into fourteen pieces, and threw them into the Nile. Isis collected thirteen of the body parts and bandaged the body making the first mummy. Osiris was transformed and became the ruler of the underworld, a state of semiconsciousness.

This legend hardly parallels the resurrection of Christ. Osiris is not resurrected from death to life. Instead, he is changed into another form and lives in the underworld in a zombie state. Christ rose physically from the grave, conquering sin and death. The body that was on the cross was raised in glory.

The legend of Attis was popular in the Hellenistic world. According to this legend, Cybele, also known as the mother goddess, fell in love with a young Phrygian shepherd named Attis. However, he was unfaithful to her, so she caused him to go mad. In his insanity, he castrated himself and died. The great mourning of Cybele caused death to enter into

---

[18]   Norman Anderson, *Christianity and World Religions* (Downers Grove, IL: InterVarsity Press, 1984), 53.

[19]   Nash, 171-72.

the world. Cybele then preserved the dead body of Attis, allowing his hair to grow and little finger to move. In some versions, Attis returns to life in the form of an evergreen tree. There is no bodily resurrection to life. All versions teach that Attis remained dead. Any account of a resurrection of Attis does not appear till 150 years after Christ.[20]

Myths of a Virgin Birth

Parallels between virgin births in the mystery religions and the virgin birth of Christ quickly break down when the facts are analyzed. In the pagan myths, the gods lust after mortal women, take on human form, and enter into physical relationships. Also, the offspring that are produced are half-human and half-divine beings. This contrasts to Christ, who was fully human and fully divine, the creator of the universe who existed from eternity past.

The alleged parallels to the virgin birth are found in the legends of Dionysus and Mithras. Dionysus is the god of wine. In this story, Zeus discovers a beautiful woman on earth named Semele. Disguising himself as a man, he has relations with her, and she becomes pregnant. Hera, Zeus's wife, in a jealous rage, attempts to burn Semele. Zeus rescues the fetus, sewing the fetus into his thigh until Dionysus is born. The birth of Dionysus is the result of a sexual union of Zeus, in the form of a man, and Semele. This is in no way a virgin birth.

One of the popular cults of the later Roman Empire was the cult of Mithra, which originated in Persia. Mithra was supposedly born when he emerged from a rock, carrying a knife and a torch and wearing a Phrygian cap. He battled first with the sun, and then with a primeval bull, thought to be the first act of creation. Mithra slew the bull, which then became the ground of life for the human race.[21] The birth of Mithra from a rock, born fully-grown, hardly parallels the virgin birth of Christ.

There is a belief that the story of Mithra contains a death and resurrection. However, there is no teaching in early Mithraism of either his death or his resurrection. Nash stated, "Mithraism had no

---

[20] Lee Stobel, *The Case for the Real Jesus* (Grand Rapids, MI: Zondervan Publishing, 2007), 177.

[21] Nash, 144.

concept of the death and resurrection of its god and no place for any concept of rebirth—at least during its early stages ... Moreover, Mithraism was basically a military cult. Therefore, one must be skeptical about suggestions that it appealed to nonmilitary people like the early Christians."[22]

Moreover, Mithraism flowered after Christianity, not before, so Christianity could not have been copied from Mithraism. The timing is incorrect to have influenced the development of first-century Christianity. It is most likely that Christianity influenced Mithraism. Edwin Yamauchi, one of the foremost scholars on ancient Persia and Mithraism states, "The earliest Mithraea are dated to the early second century. There are a handful of inscriptions that date to the early second century, but the vast majority of texts are dated after AD 140. Most of what we have as evidence of Mithraism comes in the second, third, and fourth centuries AD. That's basically what's wrong with the theories about Mithraism influencing the beginnings of Christianity."[23]

The claim that Christianity adopted its basic tenets from pagan mystery religions is false. The alleged parallels to the story of Christ are incorrect when the facts are studied. The doctrines of Christianity come from Judaism and were foreign to the mystery religions.

Conclusion

At the beginning of this study, we examined the claims of Christ. We realized there are four possible conclusions: liar, lunatic, legend, or Lord. Since the first three were inconceivable, we needed to see if Christ could further confirm His credentials of being God. We discovered that His claims were confirmed by His miracles, the record of prophecy, His sinless life, His amazing impact, and His mastery over death. Jesus proves Himself to be unique among all men.

---

[22]   Ibid., 144.
[23]   Strobel, 169.

CHAPTER 8

See the Risen Savior

With each funeral I attend, the heartache of saying good-bye to a loved one is a reminder of the reality of death. Experiencing the sadness of friends and family members reminds each one of us of our mortality and the brief moment we have here upon this earth. However, with each funeral, heaven also becomes more real to me. Each funeral reminds me that eternity's door is just a few steps away for each one of us. There is then not only a mixed heartache from the loss of a friend, but also the joyful hope that for those who know Jesus Christ, we will meet again on the other side of eternity's door.

One of the questions I often get asked by skeptics is, "How do you know heaven and hell are real? Isn't heaven just wishful thinking created by religion?" In response, I say, "We can have confidence that there is life beyond the grave because of the resurrection of Jesus Christ." The resurrection of Jesus is one of the greatest miracles He accomplished, and it has tremendous ramifications.

An Amazing Prediction

One of the most amazing predictions Jesus made was the foretelling of His death and resurrection. In John 2, Jesus was upset at the corruption He saw displayed at the Temple of Jerusalem. The Jewish leadership were profiting from religion by exploiting those who came to worship the Lord. Jesus, filled with anger, overturned the tables and chased out the moneychangers and the merchants in the courtyard and gave them a stern rebuke. The Jewish leaders, seeing this, questioned Jesus. The passage in John 2:18–22 reads:

> So the Jews said to him, "What sign do you show us for doing these things?" Jesus answered them, "Destroy this temple, and in three days I will raise it up." The Jews then said, "It has taken forty-six years to build this temple, and will you raise it up in three days?" But he was speaking about the temple of his body. When therefore he was raised from the dead, his disciples remembered that he had said this, and they believed the Scripture and the word that Jesus had spoken. So the Jews said to him, "What sign do you show us for doing these things?" Jesus answered them, "Destroy this temple, and in three days I will raise it up." The Jews then said, "It has taken forty-six years to build this temple, and will you raise it up in three days?" But he was speaking about the temple of his body. When therefore he was raised from the dead, his disciples remembered that he had said this, and they believed the Scripture and the word that Jesus had spoken.

The Jews wanted miraculous proof that Jesus had authority over the traditions and laws of the Jews. The evidence Jesus would present is his resurrection.

In Matthew 12, the Jews challenge Jesus, asking Him to show them a miraculous sign. Jesus knew their request was not sincere, so he rebukes their dishonesty and then states, "An evil and adulterous generation seeks for a sign, but no sign will be given to it except the sign of the prophet Jonah. For just as Jonah was three days and three nights in the belly of the great fish, so will the Son of Man be three days and three nights in the heart of the earth" (Matthew 12:39–40). Once again, Jesus predicted His death and resurrection in three days. Many men have predicted their death, but no one has ever predicted and accomplished their own resurrection. This is truly an astounding prediction Jesus made.

The Undisputed Facts

Skeptics and opponents of Christianity continue to challenge the historicity of the resurrection. Despite their attacks, the resurrection remains one of the best attested-to ancient historical events. When examining this event, we begin by presenting several facts upon which scholars on both sides of the issue agree.

First, Jesus died by means of Roman crucifixion. The Gospels describe the death of Jesus at the hands of His executioners and how He suffered the painful death of a Roman crucifixion. There are also numerous non-Christian sources that also record these facts (see previous chapters). The Jewish *Talmud*, Josephus, Tacitus, Thallus, and other historical works affirm that Jesus was crucified. This fact is not disputed. Even leading liberal scholars who deny the resurrection affirm the crucifixion of Jesus. For example, leading scholars from the Jesus Seminar, a group of liberal scholars who reject the miracles of Christ and believe that nearly 80 percent of the sayings attributed to Jesus in the Gospels are inaccurate or were never uttered by Him, affirm the crucifixion of Christ. Jesus Seminar co-founder John Dominic Crossan states, "That he [Jesus] was crucified is as sure as anything historical can ever be."[1] Likewise, Bart Ehrman states, "One of the most certain facts of history is that Jesus was crucified on orders of the Roman prefect of Judea, Pontius Pilate."[2]

Second, the tomb site of Jesus was known and was found empty on the third day. Jesus was a prominent figure in Israel, and His burial site was known by many people. In fact, Matthew, Mark, and John record the exact location of Jesus's tomb. Matthew wrote, "And Joseph of Arimathea took the body and wrapped it in a clean linen cloth and laid it in his own new tomb" (Matthew 27:59). Mark asserts that Joseph was a prominent member of the ruling council (Mark 15:43). It would have been destructive for the writers to invent a man of such prominence, name him specifically, and designate the tomb site since eyewitnesses would have easily discredited the author's fallacious claims.

---

[1]   John Dominic Crossan, *Jesus: A Revolutionary Biography* (San Francisco, CA: Harper Collins Publishers, 1989), 145.

[2]   Bart Ehrman quoted in Michael Licona, *The Resurrection of Jesus* (Downers Grove, IL.: InterVarsity Press, 2010), 600.

Jewish and Roman sources both testify to an empty tomb. Matthew 28:12–13 specifically states that the chief priests invented the story that the disciples stole the body. There would be no need for this fabrication if the tomb had not been empty. Opponents of the resurrection must account for this. If the tomb had not been empty, the preaching of the apostles would not have lasted one day. To put an end to Christianity, the Jewish authorities only needed to produce the body of Jesus. However, this was never done.

Along with the empty tomb is the fact that the corpse of Jesus was never found. There are no historical records from the first or second century attacking the factuality of the empty tomb or claiming discovery of the corpse. Tom Anderson, former president of the California Trial Lawyers Association, states:

> Let's assume that the written accounts of His appearances to hundreds of people are false. I want to pose a question. With an event so well publicized, don't you think that it's reasonable that one historian, one eyewitness, one antagonist would record for all time that he had seen the body? ... The silence from history is deafening when it comes to the testimony against the resurrection.[3]

Third, we have to account for the changed lives of the apostles. The Gospels record that while Jesus was on trial, the apostles deserted Him in fear. However, just a few days later, the disciples suddenly returned to Jerusalem and began preaching that Jesus was the Messiah of the Jews and that He has risen from the dead. All the men knew this message would bring them a life of suffering and even death. What accounts for this sudden transformation? Ten out of the eleven apostles died as martyrs believing Christ rose from the dead, and John, who was not martyred, endured persecution until his death. Something very compelling must have occurred to account for this sudden transformation.

Fourth, the apostles began preaching the resurrection in Jerusalem. This is significant since this is the very city in which Jesus was crucified.

---

[3]   Josh McDowell, *The Resurrection Factor* (San Bernardino, CA.: Here's Life Publishers, 1981), 66.

This was the most hostile city in which to preach such a message, for the enemies who had crucified Christ were there in the city and were still in positions of power. Furthermore, all the evidence was there for everyone to investigate. In contrast, legends take root in foreign lands or at least three generations after the event, which makes the task of discrediting legends difficult since eyewitnesses are not present. However, in the case of the resurrection, the preaching occurs in the city of the event very shortly after it occurred. Every possible fact could have been investigated thoroughly. We can safely assume that the enemies of Christianity investigated the evidence, for they were earnestly seeking ways to discredit the teachings of the apostles.

Fifth, we must account for the massive Jewish societal transformation. Thousands of Jews in Jerusalem suddenly abandoned major tenets and practices of their faith and accepted Jesus as the Messiah who fulfilled the Law. Thousands of Jews suddenly abandoned worship on the Sabbath and began worshipping on Sunday, the day Christ rose from the grave. Numerous Jews abandoned the Temple sacrifice, believing Christ fulfilled the sacrificial laws. What is the best explanation that accounts for these significant changes among so many Jews?

Finally, one must account for the origin of the Church, which preached the resurrection from the very beginning. We know that the Gospels and Acts were written prior to 65 AD. This confirms that the message was preached from the beginning. However, we have an even earlier account. First Corinthians 15:1–9 is an early creed that dates back to within five years of the resurrection (Galatians 1:11–24). This message could not have lasted if the historicity of the resurrection could not have been defended in the face of the enemies who were seeking to discredit the message of the disciples and the early church. Anyone studying the resurrection must account for these facts.

Alternative Explanations

Those who deny the resurrection have offered alternative explanations. However, these alternatives have failed in their effort to present a viable alternative.

The Disciples Stole the Body

The oldest explanation is the stolen body theory. This explanation began the day of the resurrection and is still believed by many opponents of Christianity. Matthew 28:12–13 records the genesis of this explanation, "And when they had assembled with the elders and taken counsel, they gave a sufficient sum of money to the soldiers and said, 'Tell people, His disciples came by night and stole him away while we were asleep."

Many wonder why Matthew records this and then does not refute it. Perhaps it is because this explanation was so unrealistic that he did not see a need to do so. This explanation remains highly implausible for several reasons. First, if the soldiers were sleeping, how did they know it was the disciples who stole the body? Second, it seems physically impossible for the disciples to sneak past the soldiers and then move a two-ton stone up an incline in absolute silence. Certainly the guards would have heard something. Third, the tomb was secured with a Roman seal. Anyone who moved the stone would break the seal, an offense punishable by death. The depression and cowardice of the disciples make it difficult to believe that they would have suddenly become so brave as to face a detachment of soldiers, steal the body, and then lie about the resurrection when they would ultimately face a life of suffering and death for their contrived message. History reveals that men and women will not die for what they know and can confirm to be a lie.

Fourth, Roman guards were not likely to fall asleep on such an important assignment. There were penalties for doing so. The disciples most likely would have had to overpower them, which is a highly unlikely scenario. Finally, John records that the grave clothes of Jesus along with the burial cloth that had been around His head were found folded up neatly next to the linen (John 20:7). If the disciples kidnapped the body, they would have to sneak past the guards, roll away the stone, unwrap the body, rewrap it in their wrappings, and fold the headpiece neatly next to the linen. In a robbery of this magnitude, the men would have flung the garments down in disorder and fled quickly in fear of detection.

The Wrong Tomb Theory

A second theory is the wrong tomb theory. Proponents of this argument state that according to the Gospel accounts, the women visited the grave early in the morning while it was dark. Due to their emotional condition and the darkness, they visited the wrong tomb. Overjoyed to see that it was empty, they rushed back to tell the disciples that Jesus had risen. A few disciples, Peter and John, then ran to the tomb, and they also went to the wrong tomb and found it empty. The disciples in turn ran into Jerusalem to proclaim the resurrection.

There are several flaws to this explanation that make it a highly unlikely possibility. First, it is extremely doubtful that the apostles would not have corrected the women's error. Second, the tomb was known not only by the followers of Christ but also by their adversaries. The Gospels tell us that the body was buried in the tomb of Joseph of Arimathea, a member of the Jewish council. If the body still remained in the tomb while the apostles began preaching, the authorities simply would have to go to the right tomb, produce the body, and march it down the streets. This would have ended the Christian faith once and for all. Remember, the preaching of the resurrection began in Jerusalem, the city in which Christ was tried, crucified, and buried. These factors make this theory very weak.

The Hallucination Theory

A third theory is the hallucination theory. This theory holds that the resurrection of Christ occurred in the minds of the followers of Christ. Dr. William McNeil articulates this position in his book, *A World History:*

> The Roman authorities in Jerusalem arrested and crucified Jesus ... But soon afterwards the dispirited apostles gathered in an upstairs room and suddenly felt again the heartwarming presence of their master. This seemed absolutely convincing evidence that Jesus death on the cross had not been the end but the beginning ... The Apostles bubbled over with excitement and tried to explain to all who would listen all that had happened.[4]

---

[4]   William McNeil, *A World History* (New York: Oxford University Press, 1979), 163.

This position is unrealistic for several reasons. In order for hallucinations of this type to occur, psychiatrists agree that several conditions must exist. However, this situation was not conducive for hallucinations. First, hallucinations generally occur to people who are imaginative and of a nervous makeup. But the appearances of Jesus occurred to a variety of people. Hallucinations are subjective and individual. No two people have the same experience. In this case, over five hundred people (1 Corinthians 15) have the same account. Also, hallucinations occur only at particular times and places and are associated with the events. The resurrection appearances occur in many different environments and at different times. Finally, hallucinations of this nature occur to those who intensely want to believe. However, several, such as Thomas, Paul, and James the half brother of Jesus, were very skeptical regarding the news of the resurrection. If one continues to argue this position, they still must account for the empty tomb. If the apostles were preaching a dreamed-up resurrection, all the authorities needed to do was produce the body and that would have ended the apostles' dream. These facts make this theory extremely unlikely.

The Swoon Theory

A fourth theory espouses that Jesus never died on the cross but merely passed out and was mistakenly considered dead. After three days, He revived, exited the tomb, and appeared to His disciples, who believed He had risen from the dead. This theory was developed in the early nineteenth century, but few hold to this theory presently.

There are several problems with this theory. First, it is highly unlikely that Jesus could have survived the tortures of the crucifixion. Second, the soldiers who crucified Jesus were experts in executing this type of death penalty. They could recognize a dead person from one who may have been unconscious. Furthermore, they took several precautions to make sure He was dead, one of which is that they thrust a spear into His side. When blood and water come out separately, this indicates the blood cells have begun to separate from the plasma, which will only happen when the blood stops circulating. Upon deciding to break the legs of the criminals (in order to speed up the process of dying), they carefully examined the body of Jesus and found that He was already dead.

After being taken down from the cross, Jesus was covered with eighty pounds of spices and embalmed. It is unreasonable to believe that after three days with no food or water, Jesus would revive. Even harder to believe is that Jesus could roll a two-ton stone up an incline, overpower the guards, and then walk several miles to Emmaus. Even if Jesus had done this, His appearing to the disciples half-dead and desperately in need of medical attention would not have prompted their worship of Him as God.

In the nineteenth century, David F. Strauss, an opponent of Christianity, put an end to any hope in this theory. Although he did not believe in the resurrection, he concluded this theory to be a very outlandish one. He stated:

> It is impossible that a being who has been stolen half-dead out of the sepulcher, who crept about weak and ill, wanting medical treatment, who required bandaging, strengthening, and indulgence, and who still at last yielded to his sufferings, could have given the disciples the impression that he was a conqueror over death and the grave, the Prince of life, an impression which lay at the bottom of their future ministry.[5]

Wild Dogs Ate the Body Theory

John Dominic Crossan, a prominent leader of the Jesus Seminar, has introduced a recent theory. He argues that the body of Jesus was thrown in a shallow grave and was later dug up and eaten by wild dogs. He writes:

> If the Romans did not observe the Deuteronomic decree, Jesus' dead body would have been left on the cross for wild beasts. And his followers who had fled would know that. If the Romans did observe the decree, the soldiers would have made certain Jesus was dead and then buried him themselves as part of their job. In either

---

5 David Strauss, *The Life of Jesus for the People*, Vol. 1 2nd edition (London: Williams and Norgate, 1879), 412, quoted in Josh McDowell, *The Resurrection Factor* (San Bernadino, CA.: Here's Life Publishers, 1981), 98-9.

case his body left on the cross or in a shallow grave barely covered with dirt and stones, the dogs were waiting. And his followers who had fled, would know that too.[6]

There are several problems with this recent theory. First, it is significant to note that this theory was not proposed until recent times, two thousand years after the fact. Eyewitness opponents of Christianity never mentioned this as a possible explanation but instead offer an explanation that the disciples stole the body while the guards slept. This alternative would not be necessary if people knew the fate of Jesus' body. The Gospel writers also go to great lengths to identify the tomb site. They name the owner, Joseph of Arimathea.

Crossan counters this by suggesting that the disciples created this fictitious character:

> The dilemma is painfully clear. Political authority had crucified Jesus and was against him. But, his followers knew, it also took authority or at least authority's permission to bury him. How could one have it both ways? ... Mark 15:42–46 solves the problem by creating one Joseph of Arimathea.[7]

As indicated earlier, it would have been disastrous for the Gospel writers to make up a fictional character and give him such a high-profile position in society. This fact could have easily been researched and confirmed or discredited by eyewitnesses. On top of this, the disciples would have to invent the account of the guards at the tomb, which would only compound their problems. Crossan's argument is not consistent with the facts and not a reasonable option.

The Substitution Theory

The *Quran* rejects the death, burial, and resurrection of Jesus Christ because Muslims believe that Allah would not allow His prophet to die such a shameful kind of death. The *Quran* teaches that Jesus did not die on the cross. Sura 4:157–159 states:

---

[6]   John Dominic Crossan, *Jesus, a Revolutionary Biography* (San Francisco: Harper Collins Publishers, 1989), 154.

[7]   Ibid., 156.

That they said (in boast), 'We killed Christ Jesus the son of Mary, the Apostle of God';—But they killed him not, nor crucified him, but so it was made to appear to them, and those who differ therein are full of doubts, with no (certain) knowledge, but only conjecture to follow, for of a surety they killed him not:—Nay, God raised him up unto Himself; and God is exalted in power, wise;—And there is none of the people of the Book but must believe in him before his death; And on the Day of Judgment He will be a witness against them.

Muslims believe that Jesus did not die on the cross but escaped death and was taken up to heaven. The phrase, "God raised him ..." (Acts 10:40), is understood to teach that Jesus was taken up alive to heaven, never experiencing death. Based on the phrase, "made him to appear" (Acts 10:40), orthodox Muslims have traditionally interpreted this to mean that God made someone else look like Jesus, and this person was crucified instead of Christ. There are various views regarding the identity of this substitute. Candidates include Judas, Simon of Cyrene, or a teenage boy.

The *Quran's* account is not built on historical evidence but rather a commitment to Muslim theology. There is little historical evidence to support the *Quran* in its denial of the crucifixion and resurrection and its assertion that someone else took Jesus' place on the cross. To support their view, Muslims often appeal to the "Lost Gospels." These are the Gnostic Gospels such as the *Gospel of Judas* and others. However, these have proven to be non-apostolic works, written centuries after the life of the apostles. They are not regarded as historically accurate and were written by Gnostics attempting to refashion Jesus in their image.

As demonstrated in the previous chapter, there is strong evidence to support the historicity of the Gospels and the fact that they were written by first century eyewitnesses or their close associates. Moreover, there are thousands of ancient manuscripts dated as early as the beginning of the second century, confirming that the Gospels have been accurately preserved. There are also several non-Christian, Roman, and Jewish historical works that affirm both the death of Christ and that Christians believed He had risen from the dead. These include the writings of Tacitus, Thallus, Lucian, Josephus, and the Jewish *Talmud.* Finally, the preaching of the death and resurrection of Christ began just days after His death on the cross and has been continuously preached since then for over two thousand years. This account was proclaimed from the beginning, not generations after the resurrection.

The Bible clearly teaches that Jesus predicted His death and resurrection (Matthew 26:2; Mark 10:33 and 14:8; John 2:19). This poses a serious problem for Islam's theory. If Jesus did not die and rise from the dead, Jesus was guilty of false prophecy. However, if Jesus was aware that someone else took His place on the cross, He would have been guilty of lying. So, a Muslim would have to admit, Jesus was a false prophet or a liar. However, this is something Muslims would never say about Jesus.

Muslims will state that the New Testament has been corrupted and altered. However, they have no evidence of this. The thousands of manuscripts, quotes from the Church Fathers, and translations assure us that the New Testament has been accurately preserved. Muslims have failed to expose these alleged corrupted manuscripts, which deny the death and resurrection of Jesus.

The Bible records the crucifixion, burial, and resurrection of Christ, which is central to the preaching of the apostles and to Christianity. The *Quran* and the Gospels cannot be true at the same time since they present contradictory accounts. One must examine the historical evidence and determine which account the evidence supports.

Monumental Implications

The evidence surrounding the empty tomb points to the resurrection as the best and most reasonable explanation. All alternative explanations have failed to account for the known facts. First, the resurrection of Jesus demonstrates the truth of Jesus' claims that He is indeed the divine Son of God. All the founders of the world's major religions have died, and none have conquered the grave. Muhammad lies buried in Medina. Buddha is buried in northern India. Confucius is buried in northern China. Christ alone demonstrated authority over sin and death through His resurrection. Second, the resurrection demonstrates that Jesus is the source of life and will be the judge of every person after our life here upon the earth. Third, the resurrection presents to us a living hope that death has been defeated. Eternal life in heaven is not wishful imagination but a true and living hope that is anchored in the reality of the resurrection of Christ.

CHAPTER 9

See the Word of God

There are many books today that claim to be divinely inspired. The *Quran*, the *Bhagavad Gita* (the sacred Hindu scripture), the *Book of Mormon*, and other religious works all claim to be divinely inspired. The Bible claims to be the *only* book that is divinely inspired and that all other claims of inspiration from other works should be ruled out. Does the Bible confirm its exclusive claim to be the Word of God? The totality of evidence presents a strong case for the divine inspiration of the Bible.

Testimony of the Son of God

Jesus claimed to be the divine Son of God and confirmed His claims through His miraculous life and resurrection. It has been demonstrated in previous chapters that the events of His life have been recorded accurately in the New Testament, specifically the Gospels, which have likewise proven to be historically accurate and written by first century eyewitnesses or their close associates. Since Jesus is God incarnate, whatever He taught is true, and anything opposed to His teaching is false.

Jesus directly affirmed the authority of the Old Testament and indirectly affirmed the New Testament. In Luke 11:51, Jesus identified the prophets and the canon of the Old Testament. He names Abel as the first prophet from Genesis, and Zechariah the last prophet mentioned in Second Chronicles, the last book in the Jewish Old Testament (which contains the same books we have today although placed in a different order). In Mark 7:8–9, Jesus refers to the Old Testament as the "commands of God." In Matthew 5:17, Jesus states that the "Law and the Prophets," referring to the Old Testament, is authoritative and imperishable. Throughout His ministry, Jesus made clear that His teachings, corrections, and actions were consistent with the Old Testament. The Old Testament was the standard by which He judged the teachings and traditions of others. He thus demonstrated His affirmation of the Old Testament to be the Word of God.

Jesus even specifically affirmed as historical several disputed stories of the Old Testament. He affirms as true the accounts of Adam and Eve (Matthew 19:4–5), Noah and the flood (Matthew 24:39), Jonah and the whale (Matthew 12:40), Sodom and Gomorrah (Matthew 10:15), and more.

Jesus confirmed the Old Testament and promised that the Holy Spirit would inspire the apostles in the continuation of His teaching and in the writing of what would become the New Testament (John 14:25–26 and 16:12–13). The apostles demonstrated that they came with the authority of God through the miracles they performed as Jesus and the Prophets did before them. The book of Acts, which records the miracles of the apostles, has also proven to be a historically accurate record written by a first century eyewitness.

Jesus, who proved to be the divine Son of God, affirmed the Bible to be the only divinely inspired Word of God.

Indestructibility

The Bible has been criticized, scrutinized, and attacked more than any other book. Despite the attacks upon it, it continues to uphold its authority and accuracy. Skeptics doubted its prophetic legacy, its historical accuracy, its moral teachings, and its consistency, but each time the skeptics have been shown to be wrong and the Bible continues to prove itself to be an authoritative and inspired work. Just the fact that it remains undaunted for over two thousand years, despite all the vicious attacks, demonstrates that it is a unique book. Jesus predicted the indestructibility of His words stating, "Heaven and earth will pass away, but my words will not pass away" (Matthew 24:35).

Prophecy

Many religious books claim to be divinely inspired, but only the Bible has evidence of supernatural confirmation. We have seen that Jesus, being God incarnate, affirms the inspiration of the Bible. Another evidence of supernatural confirmation is the testimony of prophecy. The biblical authors made hundreds of specific prophecies of future events that have come to pass in the manner they were predicted. No book in history can compare to the Bible when it comes to the fulfillment of prophecy. Bible prophecy is remarkable in its accuracy and its detail of future events. People are named before birth, kingdoms are described before existing, and even personal destinies are laid out before the persons are born. The Bible has an extraordinary amount of prophecies as well. J. Barton Payne records nearly 737 separate matters predicted in the Bible.[1]

Here are some examples. Ezekiel, which was written in 587 BC, predicted the destruction of Tyre, a city made up of two parts: a mainland port city and an island city half a mile offshore. The prophecy states:

> Behold, I am against you, O Tyre, and will bring up many nations against you, as the sea brings up its waves. They shall destroy the walls of Tyre and break down her towers, and I will scrape her soil from her and make her a bare rock. She shall be in the midst of the sea a place for the spreading of nets, for I have spoken, declares the Lord God. And she shall become plunder for the nations, and her daughters on the mainland shall be killed by the sword. Then they will know that I am the Lord." It further states, "They will plunder your riches and loot your merchandise. They will break down your walls and destroy your pleasant houses. Your stones and

---

[1]   J. Barton Payne, *Encyclopedia of Biblical Prophecy* (New York: Harper and Row, 1973), 681.

timber and soil they will cast into the midst of the water (Ezek. 26:3–6, 12).

Ezekiel prophesied that Nebuchadnezzar would destroy the city, many nations would fight against her, the debris of the city would be thrown into the ocean, the city would never be found again, and fishermen would come there to lay their nets. In 573 BC, Nebuchadnezzar destroyed the mainland city of Tyre. Many of the refugees of the city sailed to the island, and the island city of Tyre remained a powerful city. In 333 BC, however, Alexander the Great laid siege to Tyre. Using the rubble of mainland Tyre, he built a causeway to the island city of Tyre. He then captured and completely destroyed the city. In 314 BC, the city was rebuilt, but in 1291 AD the Muslims destroyed it.

Today, Tyre is a small fishing town where fishing boats come to rest and fisherman spread their nets on the bare rock that was once the great city. The great ancient city of Tyre to this day lies buried in ruins exactly as prophesied. If we were to calculate the odds of this event happening by chance, the figures would be astronomical. It was not by coincidence this prophecy was so accurately fulfilled.[2]

The book of Daniel is an amazing book of prophecy. Written in the sixth century BC, Daniel predicted the future empires of Persia, Greece, and Rome (Daniel 2 and 7). Daniel also accurately predicted the rise and sudden fall of Alexander the Great. He then, in great detail, described the successors and future events of the Greek Empire, predicting the coming of Antiochus Epiphanes and the sacrilegious act he would perform in the Jerusalem Temple in 168 BC (Daniel 11). In chapter nine, Daniel predicted the exact day that the Jewish Messiah would be killed (9:24–27).[3]

Jeremiah and Obadiah, written in the sixth century BC, predicted the destruction of the Edomites, who dwelt in modern day Jordan. They built their dwellings in the cliffs, making themselves nearly an impenetrable fortress civilization. However, both Obadiah and Jeremiah

---

[2]   Ralph H. Alexander, "Ezekiel," in *The Expositor's Bible Commentary*, ed. Frank E. Gaebelein (Grand Rapids: Zondervan, 1986), 869.

[3]   John Walvoord, *Daniel: The Key to Prophetic Revelation* (Chicago: Moody Press, 1971), 252-80.

49:1–8 predicted the destruction of the Edomites, even though they lived high in the cliffs in impenetrable dwellings. Indeed, the Edomites were conquered by the Naboteans in fifth century BC. Later, Rome invaded and captured their land. In 636 AD, the Muslims destroyed the city, and it remains uninhabited to this day. It was a lost civilization until it was discovered in 1812.

The prophet Ezekiel made some amazing prophecies. In chapter 44:1–3, he states that the eastern wall of Jerusalem will remain shut till Christ returns. In 1513, Sultan Suleiman the Great blocked the gate, not knowing he had inadvertently fulfilled Bible prophecy. When you visit Jerusalem today, there is a Muslim grave in front of the Eastern wall that remains sealed shut.

Jeremiah 31:35–36 states:

> Thus says the LORD, who gives the sun for light by day and the fixed order of the moon and the stars for light by night, who stirs up the sea so that its waves roar—the LORD of hosts is his name: "If this fixed order departs from before me," declares the LORD, "then shall the offspring of Israel cease from being a nation before me forever."

In other words, the people of Israel will not cease to be a nation until the Lord returns. Imagine telling the ruler of the golden Babylonian Empire that this little nation of Israel, whose capital city he destroyed and the people he deported, will long outlive his Empire. One day the Babylonian Empire will cease, but Israel will live on. I am sure the king would have laughed at this thought. Likewise, imagine telling the Emperor of Rome that the tiny nation of Israel would long outlive the powerful Roman Empire. This claim would have been met with the same skepticism. Empires have risen and fallen, but Israel remains. The fact that this nation has remained for four thousand years is a testimony to Bible prophecy.

There are over one hundred prophecies made about Jesus in the Old Testament regarding His place of birth, how He would die, His rejection by the nation of Israel, and so on. All these prophecies were made hundreds of years before Jesus ever came to earth. Because of the accuracy of the prophecies, many skeptics have believed that they must have been written after AD 70, after the death of Jesus and the destruction of Jerusalem. They have thereby tried to deny that they are even prophecies.

There was strong evidence that the Old Testament canon was completed by 450 BC. The Greek translation of the Old Testament, the *Septuagint,* is dated about 250 BC. The translation process occurred during the reign of Ptolemy Philadelphus who ruled from 285 to 246 BC.[4] We can conclude that a complete Hebrew text, from which the Greek translation would build upon, must have existed prior to the third century BC.

The Dead Sea Scrolls, discovered in 1947, provided further proof that the Old Testament canon existed prior to the third century BC. Thousands of manuscript fragments from all the Old Testament books except Esther were found predating Christ's birth with some dating as early as the third century BC.[5] Fragments from Daniel (4QDan[c]), date to the second century B.C.[6] Portions from the twelve minor prophets of the Old Testament (Manuscript 4QXII) date from 150 BC to 25 BC.[7]

One of the most important scrolls found is the Isaiah Scroll (1QIsa). This twenty-four-foot scroll was well-preserved and contains the complete book of Isaiah. This scroll was dated 100 BC and contains one of the clearest and most complete prophecies of the Messiah in chapter fifty-three, the "Suffering Servant." In this passage alone there are nearly a dozen prophecies of Christ, making this passage alone a truly remarkable text.

This discovery confirmed that the Old Testament prophecies of Christ were written and recorded well before Jesus was born. It would have been an incredible accomplishment for Jesus to have fulfilled the numerous prophecies. Some argue that these prophecies were fulfilled by

---

4   Norman Geisler and William Nix, *A General Introduction to the Bible,* (Chicago: Moody Press, 1986), 503-504.

5   James Vanderkam and Peter Flint, *The Meaning of the Dead Sea Scrolls,* (San Francisco, CA.: Harper Collins Publishers, 2002), 115.

6   Ibid., 137.

7   Ibid., 138-139.

chance, but the odds for this would be exceptionally large. It would take more a greater leap of faith to believe in that chance happening than in the fact that Jesus is God and these prophecies were divinely inspired.

No other book has the prophetic legacy of the Bible. The record of prophecy is thus evidence for the unique and supernatural origin of the Bible.

Unity despite Diversity

The Bible is the only book with supernatural confirmation to support its claim of divine inspiration. The testimony of Christ and the legacy of prophecy are two proofs for inspiration. A third line of evidence is the unity of the Bible.

The Bible covers hundreds of topics, yet it does not contradict itself. It remains united in its theme. "Well, what's so amazing about that?" you may ask. Consider these facts. First, the Bible was written over a span of fifteen hundred years. Second, it was written by more than forty men from every walk of life. For example, Moses was educated in Egypt, Peter was a fisherman, Solomon was a king, Luke was a doctor, Amos was a shepherd, and Matthew was a tax collector. All the writers were of vastly different occupations and backgrounds.

Third, it was written in many different places. The Bible was written on three different continents: Asia, Africa, and Europe. Moses wrote in the desert of Sinai, Paul wrote in a prison in Rome, Daniel wrote in exile in Babylon, and Ezra wrote in the ruined city of Jerusalem.

Fourth, it was written under many different circumstances. David wrote during a time of war, Jeremiah wrote at the sorrowful time of Israel's downfall, Peter wrote while Israel was under Roman domination, and Joshua wrote while invading the land of Canaan.

Fifth, the writers had different purposes for writing. Isaiah wrote to warn Israel of God's coming judgment on their sin, Matthew wrote to prove to the Jews that Jesus is the Messiah, Zechariah wrote to encourage a disheartened Israel, who had returned from Babylonian exile, and Paul wrote addressing problems in different Asian and European churches.

If we put all these factors together, the Bible was written over fifteen hundred years by forty different authors at different places, under various circumstances, and addressing a multitude of issues. It is amazing that with such diversity the Bible proclaims a unified message. That unity is organized around one theme: God's redemption of man and all of creation. The writers address numerous controversial subjects, yet contradictions never appear. The Bible is an incredible document.

Let me offer you a good illustration. Suppose ten medical students, graduating in the same year from medical school, wrote position papers on four controversial subjects, such as euthanasia, homosexuality, abortion, and cloning. Would they all agree on each point? No, there would be disagreements between one author and the next. In contrast, regarding the authorship of the Bible, all of these authors, over a span of fifteen hundred years, wrote on many deep theological, philosophical, and controversial subjects, yet they do not contradict one another.

It seems one author guided these writers through the whole process: the Holy Spirit. Second Peter 1:21 states, "For no prophecy was ever produced by the will of man, but men spoke from God as they were carried along by the Holy Spirit." The unity of the Bible is just one more amazing proof of the divine inspiration and authority of the Bible.

Archaeology

We've studied the testimony of Jesus, prophecy, and the unity of the Bible as providing supernatural confirmation of the Bible. Another line of evidence is archaeology. Archaeology demonstrates the historical reliability of the Bible, which is an essential part of inspiration. If the Bible is the Word of God, we would expect it to accurately reflect truth in its historical record.

Middle Eastern archaeological investigations have proven the Bible to be true and unerringly accurate in its historical descriptions. Nelson Glueck, a renowned Jewish archaeologist, states, "No archaeological discovery has ever controverted a biblical reference."[8] Dr. William

---

8   Nelson Glueck, *Rivers in the Desert: A History of the Negev* (New York: Farrar, Strauss, and Cudahy, 1959), 31, quoted in Norman Geisler, *Baker Encyclopedia of Christian Apologetics* (Grand Rapids, MI: Baker Books, 1999), 95.

Albright, who was probably the foremost authority in Middle East archaeology in his time, said this about the Bible: "There can be no doubt that archaeology has confirmed the substantial historicity of the Old Testament."[9] Both renowned archaeologists made these comments in the twentieth century. At this time in the early twenty-first century, the number of archaeological discoveries that relate to the Bible number in the hundreds of thousands.[10]

Archaeology has verified numerous ancient sites, civilizations, and biblical characters whose existence was questioned by the academic world and often dismissed as myths. Biblical archaeology has silenced many critics as new discoveries supported the facts of the Bible. Here are a few examples of the historical accuracy of the Bible. Chapter Six examined the Gospels and provided much New Testament archaeology, so I here will focus on Old Testament archaeology.

The Hittite Empire

The Hittites played a prominent role in Old Testament history. They interacted with biblical figures as early as Abraham and as late as Solomon. They are mentioned in Genesis 15:20 as people who inhabited the land of Canaan. First Kings 10:29 records that they purchased chariots and horses from King Solomon. The most prominent Hittite is Uriah, the husband of Bathsheba. The Hittites were a powerful force in the Middle East from 1750 BC until 1200 BC. Prior to the late nineteenth century, nothing was known of the Hittites outside the Bible, and many critics alleged that they were an invention of the biblical authors.

In 1876, a dramatic discovery changed this perception. A British scholar named A. H. Sayce found inscriptions carved on rocks in Turkey. He suspected that they might be evidence of the Hittite nation. Ten years later, more clay tablets were found in Turkey at a place called Boghaz-koy. German cuneiform expert Hugo Winckler investigated the tablets and began his own expedition at the site in 1906.

---

9   William F. Albright, *Archaeology and the Religion of Israel* (Baltimore: John Hopkins, 1953), 176.
10 Randall Price, *The Stones Cry Out* (Eugene, OR.: Harvest House Publishers, 1997), 25.

Winckler's excavations uncovered five temples, a fortified citadel, and several massive sculptures. In one storeroom, he found over ten thousand clay tablets. One of the documents proved to be a record of a treaty between Ramses II and the Hittite king. Other tablets showed that Boghaz-koy was the capital of the Hittite kingdom. Its original name was Hattusha and the city covered an area of three hundred acres. The Hittite nation had been discovered!

Less than a decade after Winckler's find, Czech scholar Bedrich Hronzny proved the Hittite language is an early relative of the Indo-European languages of Greek, Latin, French, German, and English. The Hittite language now has a central place in the study of the history of the Indo-European languages.[11]

The discovery also confirmed other biblical facts. Five temples were found containing many tablets with details of the rites and ceremonies that priests performed. These ceremonies described rites for purification from sin and purification of a new temple. The instructions proved to be very elaborate and lengthy. Critics once criticized the laws and instructions found in the books of Leviticus and Deuteronomy as too complicated for the time it was written (1400 BC). The Boghaz-koy texts, along with others from Egyptian sites and a site along the Euphrates called Emar, have proven that the ceremonies described in the Jewish Pentateuch are consistent with the ceremonies of the cultures of this time period.[12]

The Hittite Empire made treaties with civilizations they conquered. Two dozen of these have been translated and provide a better understanding of treaties in the Old Testament. The discovery of the Hittite Empire at Boghaz-koy has significantly advanced our understanding of the patriarchal period. Dr. Fred Wright summarizes the importance of this find in regard to biblical historicity:

Now the Bible picture of this people fits in perfectly with what we know of the Hittite nation from the monuments. As an empire they never conquered the land of Canaan itself, although the Hittite local tribes did settle there at an early date. Nothing discovered by the

---

[11]   Price, 83.
[12]   Ibid., 83-4.

excavators has in any way discredited the Biblical account. Scripture accuracy has once more been proved by the archaeologist.[13]

The discovery of the Hittites has proven to be one of the great archaeological finds of all time. It has helped to confirm the biblical narrative and had a great impact on Middle East archaeological study. Because of it, we have come to a greater understanding of the history of our language, as well as the religious, social, and political practices of the ancient Middle East.

The Walls of Jericho

One of the stories that bothered me was the story of Jericho. Even after I became a follower of Christ, I still had trouble believing this story in Joshua. According to the Bible, the conquest of Jericho occurred in approximately 1400 BC. The miraculous nature of the conquest has caused some scholars to dismiss the story as folklore. Throughout high school and college, I was taught that this was a mythical fairy tale. However, when I began to investigate the evidence, I discovered some very interesting facts.

Over the past century, four prominent archaeologists have excavated the site: Carl Watzinger from 1907–1909, John Garstang in the 1930s, Kathleen Kenyon from 1952–1958, and currently Bryant Wood. The result of their work has been eye-opening.

First, they discovered that Jericho had an impressive system of fortifications. Surrounding the city was a retaining wall fifteen feet high. At its top was an eight-foot brick wall strengthened from behind by an earthen rampart. Domestic structures were found behind this first wall. It is believed that the lower class inhabitants dwelt in the area. It is believed that Rahab, the harlot who helped the Jewish spies, dwelt in this section of the city (Joshua 2:15). Behind this segment of the city was a second brick wall, which enclosed the inner section of the city.

Archeologists found that, in one part of the city, large piles of bricks were found at the base of both the inner and outer walls indicating a sudden collapse of the fortifications. Scholars feel that an earthquake,

---

[13] Fred Wright, *Highlights of Archaeology in the Bible Lands*, (Chicago: Moody Press, 1955), 94-95.

which may also explain the damming of the Jordan in the biblical account, caused this collapse. The collapsed bricks formed a ramp by which an invader might easily enter the city (Joshua 6:20). Of this amazing discovery, Garstang states, "As to the main fact, then, there remains no doubt: the walls fell outwards so completely, the attackers would be able to clamber up and over the ruins of the city."[14] This is remarkable because city walls fall inward, not outward.

A thick layer of soot indicates that the city was destroyed by fire as described in Joshua 6:24. Kenyon described it this way, "The destruction was complete. Walls and floors were blackened or reddened by fire and every room was filled with fallen bricks."[15] Archaeologists also discovered large amounts of grain at the site. This is again consistent with the biblical account that the city was captured quickly. If it had fallen as a result of a siege, the grain would have been used up. This is consistent with Joshua 6:17which states that the Israelites were forbidden to plunder the city but had to destroy it totally, thus accounting for the large amount of grain.

Although the archaeologists agreed Jericho was violently destroyed, they disagreed on the date of the conquest. Garstang held to the biblical date of 1400 BC while Kenyon believed the destruction occurred approximately in 1550 BC. In other words, if Kenyon's date is accurate, Joshua arrived at a previously destroyed and uninhabited Jericho.[16] This earlier date would pose a serious challenge to the historicity of the Old Testament. Things were further complicated when William Albright concluded a revised date of 1250 BC for the conquest of Canaan by the Israelites nearly two centuries after the biblical chronology.

Recent archaeology appears to clarify the issue and point to the biblical date of 1400 BC. A key discovery was the Merenptah

---

[14] John Garstang, *The Foundations of Bible History; Joshua, Judges* (London: Constable, 1931), 146, quoted in Josh McDowell, *The New Evidence That Demands a Verdict* (Nashville, TN: Thomas Nelson Publishers, 1999), 382.

[15] Kathleen Kenyon and Thomas Holland, *Excavations at Jericho Vol. 3: The Architecture and Stratigraphy of the Tell*, (London: BSA), 370, quoted in Bryant Wood, "Did the Israelites Conquer Jericho? A New Look at the Archaeological Evidence," *Biblical Archaeological Review*, Vol. XVI, No. 2, (March/April 1990): 44–58.

[16] Price, 143.

Stele, or stone slab. Pharaoh Merenptah of Egypt (1237–1227) began raiding cities north of Egypt in the land of Canaan. One nation they confronted in battle was the nation of Israel.[17] This stele indicates that the Israelites were established in the land making Albright's date of invasion unlikely.

Dr. Bryant Wood, who is currently excavating the site, found that Kenyon's early date was based on faulty assumptions about pottery not found at the site. She did not find Cypriote pottery, but this imported pottery would not have been found in the poorer section of the city where she was digging. Wood analyzed the local Canaanite pottery and found them to match the pottery of the fourteenth century. His later date is also based on the discovery of Egyptian amulets in the tombs northwest of Jericho. Inscribed under these amulets were the names of Egyptian Pharaohs dating from 1500–1386 BC, showing that the cemetery was in use up to the end of the late Bronze Age (1550–1400 BC). Finally, a piece of charcoal found in the debris was carbon-14 dated to be 1410 BC. The evidence leads Wood to this conclusion: "The pottery, stratigraphic considerations, scarab data and a carbon-14 date all point to a destruction of the city around the end of the Late Bronze Age, about 1400 BC."[18] Thus, current archeological evidence supports the Bible's account of when and how Jericho fell.

House of David

One of the most beloved characters in the Bible is King David. Scripture says that he was a man after God's own heart. He is revered as the greatest of all Israelite kings, and the messianic covenant is established through his lineage. Despite his key role in Israel's history, until recently no evidence outside the Bible attested to his existence. For this reason, critics questioned the existence of a King David.

This all changed in the summer of 1993, when an archaeologist made what has been labeled as a "phenomenal" and "stunning" discovery. Dr. Avraham Biran and his team were excavating a site labeled Tell

---

[17]   Alfred Hoerth, *Archaeology and the Old Testament* (Grand Rapids, MI.: Baker Books, 1998), 228-30.

[18]   Bryant Wood, "Did the Israelites Conquer Jericho?" *Biblical Archaeological Review*, March/April, 1990, 57.

Dan, located in northern Galilee at the foot of Mt. Hermon. Evidence indicates that this is the site of the Old Testament land of Dan.

The team had discovered an impressive royal plaza. As they were clearing the debris, they discovered in the ruins the remains of a black basalt stele, or stone slab, containing Aramaic inscriptions. The stele contained thirteen lines of writing, but none of the sentences were complete. Some of the lines contained only three letters while the widest contained fourteen. The letters that remained were clearly engraved and easy to read. Two of the lines included the phrases "The King of Israel" and "House of David."

This is the first reference to King David found outside of the Bible. This discovery has caused many critics to reconsider their view of the historicity of the Davidic kingdom. Pottery found in the vicinity, along with the construction and style of writing, led Dr. Biran to argue that the stele was erected in the first quarter of the ninth century BC, about a century after the death of King David.

The translation team discovered that the inscription told of warfare between the Israelites and the Aramaens, which the Bible refers to during this period. In this find, a ruler of the Arameans, probably Hazael, is victorious over Israel and Judah. The stele was erected to celebrate the defeat of the two kings. In 1994, two more pieces were found with inscriptions which refer to Jehoram, the son of Ahab, ruler over Israel, and Ahaziah, who was the ruler over the "House of David," or Judah. These names and facts correspond to the account given in chapters eight and nine of Second Kings. The full inscription reads, "*I killed Jehoram son of Ahab king of Israel and I killed Ahaziah son of Jehoram king of the House of David.*" Dr. Hershel Shanks of *Biblical Archaeological Review* states, "The stele brings to life the biblical text in a very dramatic way. It also gives us more confidence in the historical reality of the biblical text."[19]

Once again, archaeology supports the existence of a key historical figure in the Bible. In this discovery, an enemy of Israel acknowledges the existence and lineage of King David. The use of the term "House of David" implies that there was a Davidic dynasty that ruled Israel.

---

[19] John Wilford, "Archaeologists say Evidence of House of David Found." *Dallas Morning News,* 6 August 1993, 1A.

We can conclude then that a historic King David existed. We can also conclude that the kingdoms of Judah and Israel were prominent political entities as the Bible describes. Critics long viewed the two nations as simply insignificant states.

Dr. Bryant Wood summarizes the importance of this find this way. "In our day, most scholars, archaeologist and biblical scholars would take a very critical view of the historical accuracy of many of the accounts in the Bible ... Many scholars have said there never was a David or a Solomon, and now we have a stele that actually mentions David."[20]

Sennacherib's Failed Invasion

Second Kings 19 records the invasion of Sennacherib of Assyria upon Israel. According to the biblical account, Sennacherib captured the northern territories of Israel and then invaded the southern territory of Judah. He eventually surrounded the city of Jerusalem and demanded the surrender of King Hezekiah and Israel. The righteous King Hezekiah sought the Lord in prayer, and that night, the Angel of the Lord killed 185,000 Assyrian soldiers. In horror, the Assyrians fled, Sennacherib was murdered by two of his sons, and his son Esarhaddon ruled in his place.

Many skeptics considered this another myth of the Bible. In 1830, at Sennacherib's Palace, a hexagon prism was discovered that contained the record of Sennacherib's rule, and it mentions his invasion of Israel. The prism states:

> As to Hezekiah, the Jew, he did not submit to my yoke, I laid siege to forty-six of his strong cities, walled forts, and the countless small villages in their vicinity and conquered them. ... I drove out of them 200,150 people, young and old, male and female, horses, mules, donkeys, camels, big and small cattle beyond counting, and considered them booty. Himself I made a prisoner in Jerusalem, his royal residence, like a bird in a cage. I surrounded him with earthworks in order to molest those who were leaving his city's gate. ... Thus I reduced his country, but I still increased the tribute and the ... presents due to me as his overlord, which I imposed

---

20   Price, 173.

later upon him beyond the former tribute, to be delivered annually. Hezekiah himself, whom the terror-inspiring splendor of my lordship had overwhelmed and whose irregular and elite troops which he had brought into Jerusalem, his royal residence, in order to strengthen it, had deserted him.[21]

This record affirms the invasion of Israel and the siege of Jerusalem as recorded in the Bible. It also affirms the historical figure of King Hezekiah. Most interesting is that Sennacherib does not record capturing Jerusalem and Hezekiah. He only states that he had Hezekiah surrounded like a "bird in cage." Why did Sennacherib not record his defeat if indeed he met such a devastating loss? It was not the custom of Assyrian kings to record their defeats for their posterity to read for generations to come. Sennacherib's silence testifies to his defeat as recorded in the Bible.

The Tablet of Nebo

Another discovery related to biblical history was made in the British Museum's great Arched Room, which holds nearly 130,000 Assyrian cuneiform tablets. Among the tablets, some of which date back nearly five thousand years, one tablet in particular, measuring only 2.13 inches wide or about the size of a small cigarette pack, was recently translated by Assyriologist and Professor from the University of Vienna, Dr. Michael Jursa. This cuneiform tablet was dated to 595 BC, or the tenth year of the reign of Nebuchadnezzar.

When deciphered, it named a high-ranking official of Babylonian King Nebuchadnezzar named *Nebo-Sarsekim*. Nebo-Sarsekim is also named in the Book of Jeremiah 39:1–3. The passage reads:

This is how Jerusalem was taken: In the ninth year of Zedekiah king of Judah, in the tenth month, Nebuchadnezzar king of Babylon marched against Jerusalem with his whole army and laid siege to it. And on the ninth day of the fourth month of Zedekiah's eleventh year, the city wall was broken through. Then all the officials of the king of

---

[21] Hoerth, 349–50.

Babylon came and took seats in the Middle Gate: Nergal-Sharezer of Samgar, **Nebo-Sarsekim** a chief officer, Nergal-Sharezer a high official and all the other officials of the king of Babylon. (emphasis added, NIV)

Jeremiah identifies Nebo-Sarsekim as a chief officer of Nebuchadnezzar who was with the King at the siege of Jerusalem in 587 BC. Jeremiah records that several of Nebuchadnezzar's top officials took seats in the Middle Gate once they broke through the walls of Jerusalem.

The Assyrian tablet identifies Nebo-Sarsekim as the chief eunuch of Nebuchadnezzar, thus confirming Jeremiah's reference. The full translation of the tablet reads:

(Regarding) 1.5 minas (0.75 kg or 1.65 pounds) of gold, the property of **Nabu-sharrussu-ukin,** the chief eunuch, which he sent via Arad-Banitu the eunuch to [the temple] Esangila: Arad-Banitu has delivered [it] to Esangila. In the presence of Bel-usat, son of Alpaya, the royal bodyguard, [and of] Nadin, son of Marduk-zer-ibni. Month XI, day 18, year 10 [of] Nebuchadnezzar, king of Babylon (emphasis added).[22]

The tablet is the financial record of Nebo-Sarsekim's gift of gold given to the Temple of Esangila, which was located in the fabled Hanging Gardens of Babylon.[23] This financial transaction took place in the tenth year of the reign of Nebuchadnezzar while Nabu-Sarsekim was serving as the chief officer to Nebuchadnezzar. This was nine years before the siege of Jerusalem. Dr. Jursa states, "It's very exciting and very surprising. Finding something like this tablet, where we see

---

[22] Nigel Reynolds, "Tiny Tablet Provides Proof for Old Testament," Telegraph. co.uk., 13 July 2007,http://www.telegraph.co.uk/news/main.jhtml;jsessionid= OE1Y2OKKNRS3PQFIQMFSFFWAVCBQ0IV0?xml=/news/2007/07/11/ ntablet111.xml

[23] Dalya Alberge, "Museum's tablet lends new weight to Biblical truth," *The Times* 11 July 2007, http://www.timesonline.co.uk/tol/comment/faith/article2056362. ece

a person mentioned in the Bible making an everyday payment to the temple in Babylon and quoting the exact date, is quite extraordinary."[24]

The significance of this discovery is that the Tablet of Nebo is a text outside of the Bible that confirms Jeremiah's record of Nebo-Sarsekim as a historical figure. Nebo-Sarsekim is not a prominent figure, but the fact that Jeremiah was accurate on details such as these adds considerable credibility to the Book of Jeremiah. If a writer is accurate on minor details like this, we can be confident that other recorded events, which may not have archaeological confirmation, are also true. Dr Irving Finkel, assistant keeper in the Department of the Middle East stated, "This is a fantastic discovery, a world-class find. If Nebo-Sarsekim existed, which other lesser figures in the Old Testament existed? A throwaway detail in the Old Testament turns out to be accurate and true. I think that it means that the whole of the narrative [of Jeremiah] takes on a new kind of power."[25]

This discovery of the Tablet of Nabu is yet another among thousands of archaeological findings that confirm characters, places, and events mentioned in the Bible. Not only are major historical figures confirmed, many minor characters, such as Nebo-Sarsekim and others, also have been confirmed. Dr. Geza Vermes, the eminent emeritus professor of Jewish studies at the University of Oxford, said that such a discovery revealed that "the Biblical story is not altogether invented." He added, "This will be interesting for religious people as much as historians."[26]

When a work has so much historical and archaeological confirmation, particularly when it comes to minor details, we can be confident that it is indeed a very accurate historical document. Discoveries such as this tablet continue to confirm the Bible's historical accuracy. Therefore, we can have greater confidence in the historical nature of the events where we may not have extra-biblical corroboration.

---

[24]   Ibid.
[25]   Nigel Reynolds, "Tiny Tablet Provides Proof for Old Testament," *Telegraph.co.uk.*, 13 July 2007, http://www.telegraph.co.uk/news/main.jhtml;jsessionid=OE 1Y2OKKNRS3PQFIQMFSFFWAVCBQ0IV0?xml=/news/2007/07/11/ ntablet111.xml.
[26]   Dalya Alberge, "Museum's tablet lends new weight to Biblical truth," *The Times* 11 July 2007, http://www.timesonline.co.uk/tol/comment/faith/ article2056362.ece.

The Accuracy of Luke

Archaeology has also demonstrated the accuracy of the New Testament. One of the most well-attested-to New Testament authors is Luke. Scholars have found him to be a very accurate historian in many of his details. In the Gospel of Luke and Acts, "Luke names thirty-two countries, fifty-four cities, and nine islands without error."[27] A. N. Sherwin-White states, "For Acts the confirmation of historicity is overwhelming. ... Any attempt to reject its basic historicity must now appear absurd. Roman historians have long taken it for granted."[28]

There is no other book that has so much archaeological evidence to support its accounts. Since God is a God of truth, we should expect His revelations to present what is historically true. Archaeology presents tangible proof of the historical accuracy of the Bible.

Science Speaks

Another line of evidence comes from science. The Bible is not a scientific book; it was written pre-science. However, when it speaks about the created order, what it states is indeed true. In fact, several recent discoveries affirm truths taught in the Bible centuries ago. Here are just a few examples.

The Book of Genesis teaches that the universe had a beginning (Genesis 1:1). For nearly two hundred years, scientists believed the universe was eternal. This allowed infinite time for the Darwinian evolutionary process to occur. However, with the recent discoveries, such as the red shift, radiation afterglow, and others mentioned in Chapter Two, science is now convinced the universe has a beginning. The discovery of the red shift reveals the universe has been expanding since the Big Bang. This is taught in Isaiah 42:5. The Bible taught centuries ago that the earth was round (Isaiah 40:22) and that it hangs unsuspended or unsupported in space (Job 26:7). In contrast, some Greek cultures taught that a large man named Atlas carried the earth on his back, or that the earth was flat like a plate and rested

---

27 Norman Geisler, *Baker Encyclopedia of Christian Apologetics* (Grand Rapids, MI.: Baker Books, 1999), 47.

28 Josh McDowell, *The New Evidence That Demands a Verdict* (Nashville, TN: Thomas Nelson Publishers, 1999), 64.

on water, while some Eastern cultures taught the earth rests on the back of two giant turtles.

As I discussed in Chapter Two, the universe was custom made for human life (Psalm 8:3–4). This is now called the *Anthropic Principle*. Regarding the origin of life, the Bible teaches that the basic forms of animal life begin all at once (Genesis 1), life forms remain basically the same (Genesis 1:12, 21), and all types of life begin fully formed (Genesis 1:20–21). This has been confirmed by the Cambrian Explosion and the fossil record.

Isaiah 55:10–11 and Ecclesiastes 1:7 teach us about the hydrologic cycle, which is the cycle for rain, watering of the earth, runoff into rivers and oceans, and evaporation. The principle of isostasy, the foundation of geophysics, is mentioned in Isaiah 40:12, which speaks of God "weighing the mountains in scales, and the hills in a balance."

There are skeptics who point to alleged scientific errors in the Bible, such as the Bible speaks of the sun "rising and setting" or the sun "standing still" in Joshua 10. When we read the Bible, we must recognize that the Bible uses various figures of speech such as allegory, hyperbole, anthropomorphisms, and other types of speech. Therefore, when the Bible says the sun "stood still," it is speaking from an anthropocentric (man-centered) point of view. Even today, the weatherman on television still speaks of the sunrise and sunset.

Here are just a few of the numerous examples that could be mentioned regarding the Bible and science. Although the Bible is not a science textbook, when it describes the created order, it is accurate.

Has the Bible Been Accurately Preserved?

Skeptics and critics of the Bible often allege that the Bible has been edited and altered over the centuries and, therefore, we do not have an accurate copy of the original text. However, we have good evidence that shows our New Testament has been accurately preserved. As I explained in Chapter Six, we have an abundance of New Testament manuscripts; over five thousand that date relatively close to the lifetime of the author. If early translations and quotes from the Church Fathers are included, the number increases to over twenty-four thousand.[29] With an abundance of ancient manuscripts, historians and textual scholars can confidently discern copyist errors and arrive at a very accurate copy.

The New Testament has an abundance of manuscripts, but how about the Old Testament? The Old Testament does not have the abundance of manuscripts as the New Testament because, when books became worn through aging, scribes ceremonially buried the scrolls. Critical scholars questioned the accurate transmission of the Old Testament, but a significant discovery changed the nature of the debate.

In 1947, the most significant ancient manuscript discovery was made: the discovery of the Dead Sea Scrolls. Eleven caves were discovered to contain nearly 1,100 ancient documents, which included several scrolls and more than one hundred thousand fragments.[30] Fragments from every Old Testament book except for the Book of Esther were discovered. Other works included apocryphal books, commentaries, manuals of discipline for the Qumran community, and theological texts. The majority of the texts were written in the Hebrew language, but there were also manuscripts written in Aramaic and Greek.[31]

Among the eleven caves, Cave 1, which was excavated in 1949, and Cave 4, excavated in 1952, proved to be the most productive. Some of the significant discoveries include the Isaiah Scroll, which is a well-preserved scroll of the entire book of Isaiah. The oldest known piece of biblical Hebrew is a fragment from the book of Samuel, labeled 4Qsam[b] discovered in Cave 4, and is dated to be from the third century BC.[32] Indeed, these were the most ancient Hebrew manuscripts of the Old Testament ever found, and their contents would soon yield valuable insights to our understanding of Judaism and early Christianity.

The Dead Sea Scrolls played a crucial role in determining the accurate preservation of our present Old Testament text. With hundreds

---

[29]   McDowell, 34.

[30]   Price, 278.

[31]   Gleason Archer, *A Survey of Old Testament Introduction*, (Chicago, IL.: Moody Press, 1985), 513-517.

[32]   James Vanderkam and Peter Flint, 115.

of manuscripts from every book of the Old Testament except Esther, there are many comparisons that can be made with our present day text. Our present Old Testament text is translated from the Masoretic Text. The Masoretes were Jewish scholars who between 500 AD and 950 AD gave the final form of the text to the Old Testament. Before 1947, the oldest Masoretic Text was the Aleppo Codex which dates to 935 AD.[33]

With the discovery of the Dead Sea Scrolls, we now had manuscripts that predated the Masoretic Text by one thousand years. Scholars were anxious to see how the scroll documents would match up with the Masoretic Text. If a significant amount of differences were found, we could conclude that our Old Testament text had not been well-preserved. Critics along with religious groups, such as the Muslims and Mormons, often make the claim that the present day Old Testament had been corrupted and not well-preserved. According to these religious groups' premise, this would explain the contradictions between the Old Testament and their teachings.

After years of careful study, it has been concluded that the scrolls give substantial confirmation that our Old Testament has been accurately preserved. The Dead Sea Scrolls were found to be almost identical with our Masoretic Text. Hebrew Scholar Millar Burrows writes, "It is a matter of wonder that through something like one thousand years the text underwent so little alteration. As I said in my first article on the scroll, 'Herein lies its chief importance, supporting the fidelity of the Masoretic tradition.'"[34]

A significant comparison study was conducted with the Isaiah Scroll which was a copy of the entire book of Isaiah dated 100 BC. After much research, scholars found that the two texts were practically identical. Except for minor details, such as spelling and grammar, no variants affected the meaning of the text.

One of the most respected Old Testament scholars, Gleason Archer, examined the two Isaiah scrolls found in Cave 1 and wrote, "Even

---

[33] Price, 280.

[34] Millar Burrows, *The Dead Sea Scrolls,* (New York: Viking Press, 1955), p. 304, quoted in Norman Geisler and William Nix, *General Introduction to the Bible,* (Chicago: Moody Press, 1986), 367.

though the two copies of Isaiah discovered in Qumran Cave 1 near the Dead Sea in 1947 were a thousand years earlier than the oldest dated manuscript previously known (980 AD) they proved to be word for word identical with our standard Hebrew Bible in more than 95 percent of the text. The 5 percent of variation consisted chiefly of obviously slips of pen and variations in spelling."[35]

Despite the thousand-year gap, scholars found the Masoretic Text and Dead Sea Scrolls to be nearly identical. The Dead Sea Scrolls provided valuable evidence that the Old Testament had been accurately and carefully preserved.

The Dead Sea Scrolls proved to be one of the most significant ancient manuscript discoveries of the century. This discovery demonstrated that the Old Testament has been accurately preserved, and it confirmed the prophetic nature of the messianic prophecies of Christ.

The Bible Alone is God's Word

I have given several proofs for the divine inspiration of the Bible. These include the testimony of Jesus the divine Son of God, indestructibility, prophecy, unity, archaeology, and science. The Bible is the only book with supernatural confirmation that it is the unique Word of God. Since the Bible is the Word of God, there are several important implications. First, all other works cannot be divinely inspired. But this does not mean other works do not contain truth. All people are created in the image of God and can discover and articulate principles that are true. However, only the Bible proves to be divinely inspired by God and, therefore, other claims of divine inspiration should be ruled out.

Second, other scriptures which contradict the Bible cannot be true. The law of non-contradiction states that two contradictory statements cannot be true at the same time and in the same way. If one proposition is known to be true, its opposite must be false.

Since we have good reason to believe the Bible is the inspired word of God, any teaching that contradicts the Bible must be false. The Bible makes exclusive claims regarding God, truth, and salvation that would exclude other scriptures. The Bible teaches that any deity

---

[35] Archer, 25.

other than the God of the Bible is a false deity (Exodus 20). Jesus declared that He is the divine Son of God, the source of truth, and the only way to eternal life (John 1 and 14:6). Therefore, any book that denies these truths is false.

A look at a few works from other religions illustrates this point. The Hindu scriptures include the *Vedas* and the *Upanishads*. These books present views of God that are contrary to the Bible. The *Vedas* are polytheistic, and the *Upanishads* present a pantheistic worldview of an impersonal divine essence called Brahma, not a personal God.

The *Quran*, the holy book of Islam, denies the deity of Christ, the triune nature of God, and the atoning work of Christ on the cross (Sura 4:116, 168). These are foundational truths taught in the Bible. The *Pali Canon*, the holy scriptures of Southern Buddhism, teaches a naturalistic worldview (or pantheistic, as some schools interpret it). It also teaches salvation by works and the doctrine of rebirth. The worldview of the *Pali Canon* and its view of salvation contradict biblical teachings. Since these works contradict biblical teaching, we reject their claim to divine inspiration.

The Bible alone proves to be divinely inspired and its exclusive claims rule out the claims of other books.

CHAPTER 10

See the Answer to the Problem of Evil

I have been with friends in hospital rooms grieving over the loss of a loved one that was the result of a tragic accident or criminal act. There is very little that one can say in these types of situations. I often feel helpless as I watch and share in the pain of the individuals involved. At times like these, they inevitably struggle with questions such as "How can God let something like this happen?" "Does He care?" "Why is there suffering and evil in the world?" or "Is there any hope for our suffering?" Studying the issue and wrestling with its complexities led me to conclude that Christianity is the only system that can offer both a reasonable explanation for evil and a message of hope in the midst of suffering.

The Different Worldviews and Evil

The religions that embrace a pantheist worldview teach that all reality is reduced to what Hindus call Brahma, or the divine. "This reality—Brahma—alone exists; it is the sole reality, and there are no distinctions. Everything else is illusory. This Ultimate Reality has no personality; it is impersonal and beyond description."[1]

---

[1]   Paul Copan, *That's Just Your Interpretation* (Grand Rapids, MI.: Baker Books, 2001), 50.

Based on Hindu monism—the belief that all is one—and the premise that, other than Brahma, all is an illusion, evil must then also be an illusion. There is ultimately no distinction between good or evil. Cruelty and compassion are not ultimately different. Monism not only destroys any moral law code but also eliminates an individual's responsibility to do right and stand against wrong.[2]

Our reasoning, intuition, and experience indicate that the world is not an illusion and that there is a real distinction between good and evil. Why should we believe the monist notion that the world is an illusion when it goes against our experience and intuition? Pantheism, and the religions built on this worldview, cannot offer any reasonable explanation for evil, nor can they offer any kind of hope for those experiencing the suffering that comes from evil.

The naturalist or atheist run into a more difficult problem. In order to identify something as objectively evil, there must be an external, perfect standard of good. How can we say the birth of babies with physical defects is evil, tsunamis killing thousands of people is evil, or the massacre of a particular group of people is evil unless there is a universal standard of good by which we measure such actions and events? If there is no universal, objective moral standard, all we have are subjective opinions. It would be impossible to define an act as evil.

However, our intuition helps us to sense what is evil and expects individuals to be responsible for their actions. When we experience an unjust act or witness the suffering of innocent people, our reactions show that we are able not only to perceive what is good and evil but also that we hold all men accountable to a universal standard of good, or a universal moral law code.

C. S. Lewis did not believe in God because of the presence of evil. So how was he able to define evil? One cannot identify evil unless there is an objective and universal standard of good by which evil is measured. Where did this standard come from? In his struggle to reconcile this dilemma, C. S. Lewis said:

> As an atheist, my argument against God was that the universe seemed so cruel and unjust. But how had I got this idea of just and unjust?

---

[2]   Ibid., 55.

A man does not call a line crooked unless he has some idea of a straight line. What was I comparing this universe with when I called it unjust? ... Of course I could have given up my idea of justice by saying it was nothing but a private idea of my own. But if I did that, then my argument against God collapsed too ...[3]

Even though the other worldviews do not offer a reasonable explanation for the problem of evil, the Christian must still provide an explanation. The problem of evil and suffering is one of the toughest challenges a Christian must answer. If God exists, what accounts for all the evil in the world? If we have a God who is good, loving, and sovereign, how do we account for evil, a force contrary to His nature? In dealing with this challenge, we must address two aspects of the issue: the philosophical problem of evil and the personal problem of evil. The philosophical aspect addresses the question, "Does the existence of evil argue against the existence of God?" The personal aspect deals with the struggles that come when an individual experiences evil and suffering.

The Philosophical Problem of Evil

The Origin of Evil

In answering the problem of evil, we begin with the origin of evil. How did evil arise in a perfect world? If God is perfect and everything He created was perfect, how did evil arise in such a world? The argument goes like this:

1. God is perfect.
2. Everything that God created is perfect.
3. Evil cannot arise in a perfect world with perfect creatures.
4. But evil exists in this world.
5. Therefore, either God is not perfect, or He does not exist.

In this paradigm, premise three is incorrect. Perfect creatures can do evil. It is true that God created man perfect. The Bible states that

---

[3] C. S. Lewis, *Mere Christianity*, (New York: Macmillan Publishing, 1960) 45.

God created man in His image. This means He created man to reflect some of the moral attributes of God. A perfect being then must be able to accomplish the greatest moral act of good, which is to love. Part of being made in the image of God means man has the capacity to love, and the ability to exercise love requires free will. Free will allows man to be the only creature who can have a love relationship with God.

It is impossible for love to exist without free will. Love is not love if it is forced upon someone. In a relationship of love, the other being must exercise their free will and choose to enter into the relationship. One cannot be truly free unless there is a choice of another alternative.

Allow me to illustrate this. Suppose I were an all-powerful king. One day, as I was walking through my land, I spotted a beautiful peasant girl. Now suppose I approached her with my guards and told her, "Marry me, or I will execute your family." This poor girl really has no choice but to enter into a relationship with me. This is not a love relationship, and I would never know if she truly loved me. However, following the line of many romantic movies, suppose I dressed as a pauper, developed a friendship with her, and then asked her for her hand in marriage, thus offering her the option to reject my love and choose another. Knowing that she has many worthy suitors from whom she may choose, I can be assured that she loves me because she chose to enter into this relationship with me.

God created man with the capacity to exercise his free will and choose to obey or disobey Him. Yet, with freedom there also exists the capacity for evil. The choice not to do good or to disobey God would be evil. God then made evil possible, but man, in abusing his free will, made it actual.

For example, let's say I give one of my students the keys to my car and ask, "Could you go and pick us up a pizza?" Giving him this freedom is not evil. However, he can use his freedom for evil. He can obey my wishes, or he can choose to go drag racing on the interstate freeway. Freedom creates the potential for evil. Adam, in his freedom, chose to disobey God. Thus sin entered into the world. That event was the origin of evil. In short, God created a world in which there was the potential for evil. However, it was man who actualized evil. The paradigm of how evil arises in a perfect world is answered in this way:

1. God is perfect.
2. Everything that God created is perfect.
3. Evil can arise in a perfect world when perfect creatures with free will choose evil over good.
4. Evil exists in this world because perfect creatures chose against God's perfect command.

Why Does God Allow Evil to Exist?

The next question is, "Why does God allow evil to exist?" The paradigm looks like the following:

1. An all-powerful God could destroy evil.
2. An all-loving God would destroy evil.
3. However, evil is not destroyed.
4. Therefore, an all-loving and all-powerful God does not exist.

In this paradigm, premise three is incorrect. Premise three states evil is not destroyed, implying it will never be defeated. However, there is no way we can know this. It is possible that evil will one day be defeated at God's appointed time. An all-powerful and all-loving God guarantees that one day He will defeat evil. Therefore, the paradigm is answered in this way:

1. An all-powerful God could destroy evil.
2. An all-loving God would destroy evil.
3. However, evil is not yet destroyed.
4. Therefore, an all-loving and all-powerful God will one day defeat evil at His appointed time.

This is a logical solution, but some may ask, "Why does God allow evil to exist? Why doesn't He defeat evil now?" Though God may allow evil to exist, this does not mean He is not in control. God permits evil to persist for several reasons.

First, God allows evil to persist because He is a gracious God. Second Peter 3:9 states, "The Lord is not slow in keeping His promise, as some understand slowness. He is patient with you, not wanting anyone to perish, but everyone to come to repentance." In other words, God withholds the destruction of evil so that more who are opposed to Him can turn and receive His grace. I am glad God did not destroy evil in 1980. If He had chosen to do so, I would be in hell, eternally separated from Him today since I did not confess my faith in Christ until 1984.

Second, God must allow individuals to enjoy the fruits of their wise and good choices, but He must also allow them to suffer the consequences of their disobedience as well. This is necessary for learning to take place. In order for me to grow as a child, my parents had to allow me to make my own choices. If I made a bad choice, I needed to experience the consequences of my decision. Even though it was painful for them to watch me go through it, they had to withhold their involvement and not intervene in order for me to learn and grow. In the same way, we grow as we learn to make good choices over bad choices.

Third, we learn more from our suffering than through the prosperous times. James writes, "Consider it pure joy, my brothers, whenever you face trials of many kinds, because you know that the testing of your faith develops perseverance. Perseverance must finish its work so that you may be mature and complete, not lacking anything" (James 1:2–4). It is through our suffering that we discover the flaws in our character, thereby becoming more mature like Christ.

Hebrews 5:7–8 states, "During the days of Jesus' life on earth, he offered up prayers and petitions with loud cries and tears to the one who could save him from death, and he was heard because of his reverent submission. Although he was a son, he learned obedience from what he suffered." Even Jesus, the Son of God, learned through His suffering. If Jesus needed to learn through His suffering, how much more do we?

As one who enjoys martial arts, I enjoy easy workouts and opponents I can easily defeat. However, I grow most when I am pushed to endure pain and grapple with opponents far more skilled than I.

Unless I endure through the tough workouts and skilled opponents, I will never grow as an athlete.

The same is true for a believer in Christ. The individuals whose biographies inspire us are men and women who have endured great suffering and evil, yet have persevered and overcome. We are inspired by stories of Joni Ericson Tada, a quadriplegic who found the will to trust God and live. When you meet such individuals, you are immediately impressed by the depth and quality of their character and their unshakeable faith that gives them strength to persevere. What is remarkable most of all is the joy they possess, a joy greater than many of us will ever know.

For the Christian, there is meaning and purpose in our suffering. Despite experiencing evil and suffering, God is at work in our lives and working through the situation to bring about His purpose in our lives and in this world. Therefore, even in the midst of great evil and suffering, the Christian can still have hope and joy.

Why is there So Much Senseless Suffering?

The final challenging question is, "Why is there so much senseless suffering?" In other words, everything that God does and allows must have a good purpose; however, there is so much evil and suffering that appears to have no good purpose. The paradigm goes like this:

1. A good God has a good purpose for everything.
2. However, there is much evil and suffering that has no good purpose.
3. Therefore, an all-good and omniscient God does not exist, or He is not all-good and all-knowing.

The flaw in this paradigm is that one assumes to know all things as God does; however, this is not possible. Finite beings cannot possibly know the plans and purposes of an infinite and omniscient God. Isaiah 55:9 states, "As the heavens are higher than the earth, so are my ways higher than your ways and my thoughts than your thoughts." Often in the Bible, where evil once appeared triumphant, God turned it around to be a victory in order to accomplish His plan.

In His sovereignty and wisdom, God used evil and bad circumstances to accomplish His purpose.

In Genesis 37, Joseph is betrayed by his brothers and sold into slavery in Egypt. Despite this evil act, God used it to bring about His purpose in shaping the character of Joseph to be a future ruler who would preserve the nation of Israel during a famine. In the end, Joseph saw how God used this apparent tragedy to bring about His purpose. Genesis 50:19–21 records his words to his brothers: "Am I in the place of God? You intended to harm me, but God intended it for good to accomplish what is now being done, the saving of many lives." God overcame evil and worked through the situation to accomplish His purpose.

The cross is the greatest illustration of good coming from evil. Evil seems to have prevailed when a disciple of the Lord Jesus betrays Him, the religious rulers falsely accuse Him, and the soldiers beat Him for hours. After suffering the cruel torture of crucifixion, Jesus tastes the painful death of separation from His Father. Yet this tragic event falls right into the plan of God to bring salvation to men who trust Jesus as Lord and Savior. Consequently, God maintains His sovereignty in allowing evil to exist in order to fulfill His purpose.

Since we are not infinite and omniscient like God, we cannot always know the purpose of every event that occurs. Although we may not be able to perceive any good resulting from a tragedy, we can trust that God's perspective involves the big picture and that He is providentially working all things for good.

Will God always allow evil to exist? No. God's grace and mercy will not extend indefinitely. One day, He will execute His justice and bring evil to an end.

The Personal Problem of Evil

The philosophical problem of evil answers the intellectual challenge. For those who have experienced the cruelty of evil, we must offer answers that can bring healing amidst difficult times. There are no easy solutions or quick fixes that will instantly remove the pain one feels in such times. Even the great Christians suffered and wrestled with this issue. Yet, of all the worldviews, I believe the Christian worldview offers the most meaningful and true explanations. How does the Christian face the pain of suffering that comes from experiencing evil?

First, it is important to understand that we live in a fallen world that is suffering the consequences of sin. Man, in his freedom, has chosen to turn away, seeking to live life with no regard for God or His laws. In His grace, God does not impose His will on humans and has allowed individuals to temporarily go their own way. The Apostle John writes in First John 2:15–16:

> Do not love the world or anything in the world. If anyone loves the world, the love of the Father is not in Him. For everything in the world—the cravings of sinful man, the lust of the eyes and the boasting of what he has and does—comes not from the Father but from the world.

John is not stating that we are not to love the people in the world. Rather, he is saying the system of the world is in rebellion to God. Because we live in this fallen world, we are not immune to its effects. Jesus suffered a cruel and wicked death at the hands of unrighteous men. Each apostle of Christ suffered persecution and death, except for John who spent much of his life persecuted and his final days in prison. If the Son of God and men of God were not immune from the effects of evil and suffering, it is wrong for us to think we are supposed to be exempt.

Second, we can be strengthened and draw comfort knowing God has promised never to abandon us in our time of suffering. He remains with us through the pain and suffering. Romans 8:38 states:

> For I am convinced that neither death nor life, neither angels nor demons, neither the present nor the future, nor any powers, neither height nor depth, nor anything else in all creation, will be able to separate us from the love of God that is in Christ Jesus our Lord.

Greater yet, He understands our suffering and deeply cares for our situation. God understands because He endured the greatest pain on the cross. We do not have a God who stood by indifferently and watched from a distance as we suffered. He came down from heaven, entered into our suffering, and experienced our pain alongside us on the cross. For that reason, He can relate to us in our time of need, and we can draw strength from His presence. He cares deeply about us, especially in our moments of suffering. First Peter 5:7 calls us to "Cast all your anxiety on Him because He cares for you." God never abandons His people and wants us to draw near to Him in our time of need.

Third, God remains in control of all things, and He is at work in every situation. He has a purpose for our life that is always for His glory and our good. Romans 8:28 states, "And we know that in all things God works for the good of those who love Him, who have been called according to His purpose." No matter how bad the situation may seem, God is working in ways we often cannot see or understand to bring about His purpose in our lives, which is always for His glory and our good. Our finite and temporal minds on this side of eternity may not see the end results of God's ultimate plan for our lives.

Sometimes we need to quit demanding an explanation from God as to why this tragedy occurred in our lives and instead, like Job, learn to trust the character and hand of God. Job stated in his time of great suffering, "Though he slay me, yet will I hope in him" (Job 13:15). Job learned to trust and hope in God even though he could not understand his circumstance or the reason for his suffering. When we arrive at this point like Job, it is often then that we can leave the pain of suffering behind.

Third, be assured that our suffering is not meaningless. There are valuable lessons to be learned from suffering. God will sometimes use evil to warn us and deter us from greater evils. Pain from getting too close to fire is a good thing and prevents us from further danger. In my teenage years, I got into a minor fender bender shortly after receiving my driver's license. That experience created a healthy fear in me and has kept me from the greater evil of reckless driving.

In Second Corinthians 12:7–9, Paul prayed to the Lord to deliver him from the thorn in his side. He wrote, "Three times I pleaded with the Lord to take it away from me. But he said to me, 'My grace is sufficient for you, for my power is made perfect in weakness.' Therefore I will boast all the more gladly about my weaknesses, so that Christ's power may rest on me." There are several views on what Paul meant by the "thorn in his side." It is likely a physical ailment, but the point is that God would not answer Paul's prayer the way Paul had hoped because God was protecting him from a greater danger. Paul could have become very proud and self-sufficient, but his ailment kept him humble and dependent upon Christ.

Trials also develop our character. The mettle of a person's character is tested, refined, and sharpened only when put through the fire of difficult trials. First Peter 1:6–9 states:

> In this you greatly rejoice, though now for a little while you may have had to suffer grief in all kinds of trials. These have come so that your faith—of greater worth than gold, which perishes even though refined by fire—may be proved genuine and may result in praise, glory and honor when Jesus Christ is revealed.

People of great moral integrity, who have touched our world in significant ways, endured some of the most difficult and painful experiences of life. The world has been inspired because individuals like previously mentioned quadriplegic Joni Erickson Tada have motivated us to overcome our handicaps and live sacrificially for God and others. Likewise, the works of Corrie ten Boom, Victor Frankel, and Dietrich Bonhoeffer have impacted the lives of millions because they persevered and overcame the horror of Nazi tyranny. Abraham Lincoln endured many hardships—the death of his mother at a young age and the death of three of his four children among other tragedies. Nevertheless, these very circumstances made him a man of renowned moral character and courage. As a result of these people persevering through their pain, we have a much deeper understanding of love, courage, faith, and character. Their lives inspire us to become men and women of stronger character. For this reason, James writes:

> Consider it pure joy, my brothers, whenever you face trials of many kinds, because you know that the testing of your faith develops perseverance. Perseverance must finish its work so that you may be mature and complete, not lacking anything (James 1:2–3).

Hence, in the context of a relationship with God, our suffering is not in vain, as there is a purpose for what He allows into our lives, whether it be good or difficult. We cannot dispel the pain we experience, but we can overcome it through the power of Christ.

Finally, we have hope, knowing there is a reason for our suffering, and that one day God will defeat evil and bring an everlasting dominion of peace and justice. Although we now live in a fallen world and must endure the effects of evil, this will not always be the case. One day, God will bring an end to all evil and suffering. The pain we bear now reminds us of our need to depend upon God and not ourselves for ultimate hope and to desire the day when He will restore all things. Paul writes in Second Corinthians 4:17, "For our light and momentary troubles are achieving for us an eternal glory that far outweighs them all." Promises like these bring us hope even in the face of disheartening situations. One day, our prayers will be answered. We will either go to be with the Lord at our death, or He will return and establish His kingdom forever. Either way, the Christian is victorious.

Conclusion

I was in a debate with an atheist on a talk show. The question he posed to me was this: "If God is so powerful and loving, why does He allow so many babies to be born with physical defects and live meaningless lives of suffering?"

I paused for a moment, and then responded, "First of all, let me ask you why this is evil? Your question implies an absolute standard of good from which we have fallen short. Where did you get this ultimate standard of good?" There was a brief moment of silence, and I realized he was having difficulty with that. Then I said, "What answer do you have for this child who is suffering? All you can say is that this is a product of the Darwinian Evolutionary process. In fact, take comfort because your life is ultimately without meaning anyway. We are the product of chance, we live for a brief moment in time, you will suffer meaninglessly, and then you will become extinct. It is atheism that cannot offer any rational or meaningful answer to the suffering child."

After another moment of silence, I said, "However, as a Christian, I can offer a meaningful message of hope. Who says this child's suffering and life is meaningless? The Bible teaches there is purpose, even in our suffering. We learn not only from our suffering but also from the suffering of others. I am inspired by the lives of handicapped men and women I know. They teach me the meaning of courage, gratitude, and compassion. My life and the lives of thousands are greatly enriched because of them. Finally, for those who know Christ, their suffering will one day end and in glory. They will be fully healed of their infirmities and in the presence of Jesus. This is a meaningful message of hope only a Christian can give to those who suffer."

After a brief pause, my atheist friend asked, "Well, you gave a nice answer, but how do you know this is not just wishful thinking? How do you know this is not a false hope?" To this I smiled and responded, "I know because of the resurrection of Jesus Christ." I then went on to defend the resurrection of Christ.

It is only Christianity that can offer a reasonable answer to the problem of evil and suffering, and it is only Christianity that can present a meaningful message of hope to those in pain.

CHAPTER 11

See the Only Way to God

It had been a few weeks since I had received Jesus Christ as my Lord and savior. I now had a relationship with the creator of the universe and the assurance of eternal life. John 5:24 states, "I tell you the truth, whoever hears my word and believes him who sent me has eternal life and will not be condemned; he has crossed over from death to life." It wasn't long, however, until I faced an issue that I found to be one of the most difficult to accept as a young believer in Christ.

Growing up in the Japanese culture, I had been raised in the Japanese Buddhist tradition. From childhood, my family observed many of the Buddhist festivals and ceremonies. Not long after I had received Christ, a relative passed away and the funeral would be a Buddhist funeral. I attended the funeral and sat through the ceremony. The priest offered the incense to the statue of Buddha, offered prayers, and chanted the mantras of the Buddhist sutras. He then invited all family members and friends to offer incense at the Buddhist altar.

The next day at church my friend John asked me, "How was the funeral?" I said, "Well, it was a bit depressing and dark, but knowing my relative is in heaven made it reasonably enjoyable. It was good to see all my relatives and catch up with them." John then asked me, "Did your relative know Jesus?" I replied, "No, he was a Buddhist, and it was a Buddhist funeral." John looked troubled, put his head down, and sighed a distressing, "Oh." I asked him, "Is something wrong?"

John looked at me and with a serious tone stated, "Well, Pat, Jesus stated in John 14:6, 'I am the way, the truth, and the life. No one comes to the Father except through me.' You see, without Jesus, one cannot have eternal life. He is the only way we can receive forgiveness of sins and be with God in heaven forever." I was surprised to find out that Jesus claimed to be the only way to God. Immediately, I began to struggle with that teaching, for this would mean all those in my family who were deceased were probably separated from God forever. From what I knew, I was one of the first in my entire clan to come to know Christ. Immediately, I began to ask, "Aren't all religions essentially the same?" "What about those who never heard the Gospel? Is it fair for God to send them to hell?" "Why can't there be many ways to God?"

This was a difficult teaching that I have struggled with for most of my life as a Christian. Many Christians and non-Christians struggle with this issue of whether Jesus is the only way to eternal life. Truth is not always easy to accept, but if it is truth, I must acknowledge it no matter how difficult it may be.

This claim also runs counter to the relativism so prevalent in our world today. In the current postmodern culture, we are taught to tolerate or accept all belief systems as true. The underlying attitude is that it is wrong to judge another belief system as true or false. Christians who hold to the exclusive position that Jesus is the only way to God are often are accused of being "arrogant" and "intolerant."

The idea that there are many ways to eternal life is called pluralism. Most in western culture accept the idea that there are many ways to God. A recent article in the *Dallas Morning News* stated that 70 percent of Americans believe that many religions can lead to eternal life. Studies also revealed that 60 percent of Baptist and 80 percent of Catholics believe there are many ways to eternal life.[1]

This is one of the most debated doctrines today. I have been asked to speak on this subject in cultures all over the world, and it

---

[1] Jeffrey Weiss, "Study: Most Americans Say Many Religions Can Lead to Eternal Life," *Dallas Morning News*, 24 June 2008; available from http://www.dallasnews.com/sharedcontent/dws/dn/latestnews/stories/062408dnrelpewstudy.2f6d9020.html; Internet accessed 24 June 2008.

often draws strong emotional responses from the audiences. Is Jesus the only way to God? The most loving thing one can do is to follow the evidence wherever it leads—even if it leads to conclusions we may not like.

Pluralism: Are All Religions the Same?

Pluralism is the belief that all religions are equal and valid ways to God. There is a well-known story told in the Hindu and Buddhist scriptures. It is the story of the blind men and the elephant. The story goes as follows:

> Once upon a time a king gathered some blind men about an elephant and asked them to tell him what an elephant was like. The first man felt a tusk and said an elephant was like a giant carrot; another happened to touch the ear and said it was like a big fan; another touched its trunk and said it was a pestle; still another who happened to feel its leg, said it was like a mortar; and another, who grasped its tail siad it was like a rope. Not one of them was able to tell the king the elephant's real form.[2]

Pluralists teach this is what is happening when we look at the different religions. We are blind and know neither true reality nor the true nature of God. Therefore, we are all looking at God from different perspectives, so it appears we are teaching different things. However, we are all actually describing a different aspect of the same thing. If we could see as the king in the story, we would all realize we are in essence teaching the same thing regarding God, salvation, and the nature of man.

I was told this story and similar ones as a young boy, and it has stayed with me. I often wondered how to answer this parable, but I discovered the answer was quite simple. If you carefully reflect on the story, you realize the pluralists are claiming everyone is blind but them! They believe everyone else is blind, and they have the true and correct perspective. They are thus claiming to be objective and can

---

2   Bukkyo Dendo Kyokai, *The Teaching of the Buddha*, (Tokyo: Kosaido Printing Company, 1996), 75.

see that everyone else is wrong. The question we must ask is, "How do we know the pluralist has the right perspective and that everyone else is wrong?"

Second, since the pluralist can be objective, there exists objective truth! The objective truth is that the object in front of the blind men is not a fan or a field gun or a rope. The object is an elephant, and that is the truth.

Finally, the pluralist believes that he is right and everyone who disagrees with him is wrong. In truth, they are narrow-minded. If you do not believe me, disagree with a pluralist, and see how they respond.

I was talking with a man who claimed to be a Christian, but it was obvious he was from a very liberal persuasion. He stated in our conversation, "We allow people of all religious persuasions to speak in our chapel. We tolerate all religions and views. The only people we will not allow to speak in our chapel are Christians who believe there is only one way to God. We cannot allow intolerant and narrow-minded people like that to teach in our chapel." I paused briefly, and then asked him, "So you tolerate all views?" He responded "Absolutely! We are a tolerant school, and we want to teach our students to tolerate all beliefs!" I then asked him, "So you will tolerate all beliefs except Christians who follow the teachings of Christ?" He said, "Yes. Christians who say there is only one way give the wrong message!" I then asked again, "So you will not tolerate Christians because they disagree with you? You tolerate all people as long as they agree with you. Isn't that being narrow-minded and intolerant?" He paused for a moment, suddenly realizing his self-defeating position. I then said, "I guess you would not tolerate Jesus in your chapel, would you?" He said, "Sure, I would. He taught love and tolerance." I said, "Well, Jesus was pretty narrow in his view of salvation. He said He was the only way in John 14:6." At this, the man changed the subject, wished me a good day and left. This conversation illustrates that the pluralist believes that anyone who disagrees with his position is wrong!

Reasons to Reject Pluralism

There are several good reasons pluralism fails as a coherent belief system. First, as illustrated in the previous discussion, it is self-defeating.

The pluralist believes that he is right and anyone who disagrees with him is wrong. In this way, he is showing that he is not tolerant of all religious views. If he claims his position is true, the opposite of his position cannot be true. He is claiming knowledge of objective truth about religion that he claims no one can know. In these ways, he has a self-defeating position.

A second logical reason pluralism fails is the law of non-contradiction, which states that contradictory propositions cannot both be true at the same time and in the same sense. "A is B" and "A is not B" cannot both be true. The law of non-contradiction cannot be refuted since any attempt to refute it appeals to the use of it. To say, "I reject the law of non-contradiction, for it is false," is to apply the law of non-contradiction to what you are saying. Stating, "The law of non-contradiction is false and to believe anything contrary to my view is false," is applying the law of non-contradiction, for you are saying, "My position is true and to hold to an opposing position is false."

The law of non-contradiction is the basis of all logical thinking. We apply this law every day throughout our lives. When I introduce myself to someone and say, "I am Patrick Zukeran," I am saying that I am Patrick and not anyone else. We could not have a coherent conversation without applying this law. Imagine if you asked me, "Hi, what is your name?" and I responded, "I am Patrick Zukeran, but I am not Patrick Zukeran." If you then asked me, "What state are you from?" and I responded, "I am from Hawaii, but I am not from Hawaii," you would quickly conclude I needed some serious help. We could not have a coherent conversation without applying the law of non-contradiction. It is a universal law applied by all people. All religions present contradictory beliefs on the fundamental doctrines, so they cannot all be true at the same time. When you look at their fundamental beliefs, you soon realize they are not teaching the same thing but rather contradictory teachings. Let's look at a few examples.

Nature of God or the Ultimate

In the doctrine of God, the world religions teach contrary views. Atheists and several Buddhist schools believe there is no God or creator of the universe. Hindus and several Buddhist schools are pantheists, and they believe God is an impersonal energy or force. Shinto, Animism, and Mormonism teach polytheism, the belief in many gods. Islam teaches a unified monotheism, which states there is only one God, and Allah is His name. Islam rejects the Christian Trinity as blasphemy. Islam considers the teaching that Jesus is God's Son blasphemy. Christianity teaches a personal triune God. There is one God who is revealed in three persons: one in nature, three in person. In affirming two mutually exclusive things about God, the pluralist view ends up being rationally incoherent, violating the Law of Identity. The Law of Identity is a foundational law of logic, one of the First Principles of reasoning. It states simply: A is A. If God is triune in nature, He cannot also be non-triune in nature.

It is apparent that all religions are not teaching the same thing. Is God a personal being or a nonpersonal force? Does God exist, or is there no God? Is God triune in nature or is that blasphemy? It is not possible to say all religions are teaching the same thing.

Nature of Man

Atheists follow Darwinian Evolutionary Theory, believing that man is a material being and that there is no immaterial soul or spirit that survives the death of the physical body. Human beings are essentially evolved animals.

Hinduism believes that all is one, a belief previously mentioned called monism. Since all is one, and the divine is one with the universe, man is essentially one with the divine. We are all one with the divine and with one another. Individuality is an illusion; there is no enduring person. Man is not sinful, just ignorant of his divinity.

Swami Prabhupada wrote, "A drop of ocean water has all the properties of the ocean itself, and we, although minute particles of the Supreme Whole, have the same energetic properties as the Supreme."[3] Spiritual guru to many Hollywood stars, Deepak Chopra writes, "In reality, we are divinity in disguise, and the gods and goddesses in embryo that are contained within us seek to be fully materialized. True success is therefore the experience of the miraculous. It is the

---

[3] Bhaktivedanta Prabhupada, *Beyond Birth and Death*, (Australia: The Bhaktivedanta Book Trust, 1999), p. 5

unfolding of the divinity within us."[4] Therefore, man is not sinful; he is ignorant of his true divinity.

Buddhism teaches that there is no soul or individuality. Each person is made up of five aggregates or clusters of experiences that make up our physical form, sensation, perception, and consciousness. At death, they disperse, and parts may rejoin in a new form until each aggregate enters nirvana.[5] Man is not sinful, just ignorant of the way.

Islam teaches that man is created by Allah. Man is not sinful but weak and under Allah's judgment for disobeying His laws. Man can overcome sin by his good works.

Christianity teaches that man is created in the image of God. We are individuals made up of a material body and an immaterial soul and spirit that survive the death of the physical body. Although we are created in the image of God, we are fallen and sinful by nature.

Once again, we see that the religions are not teaching the same thing. Is man sinful or just ignorant? Is man divine in essence or a finite sinful creature? Does man have an eternal soul, or is he simply a material being? Is individuality an illusion? On this doctrine, all religions are not saying the same thing.

Destiny of Man

Atheists believe that death is the end; there is only extinction. Hinduism teaches that we are in an endless cycle of reincarnation until we attain unity with God. Man's divine essence is trapped in the body due to ignorance and bad karma. Buddhism teaches that we are in an endless cycle of rebirths until we attain nirvana, the extinguishing of all. Nirvana is not a place like heaven where one exists as a person in a state of paradise. Nirvana is a state of nothingness where one ceases all existence. Islam teaches we are judged on our works. On the day of judgment, our works will be weighed, and Allah will render His judgment. It is then men will learn of their eternal fate in hell or

---

[4] Deepak Chopra, quoted in Ravi Zacharias, *Jesus Among Other Gods* (Nashville: Word Publishing, 2000), 96.

[5] John Renard, *Responses Top 101 Questions on Buddhism* (New York: Paulist Press, 1999), 47-8.

Islamic heaven. Christianity teaches that each person's eternal destiny will be determined at death (Hebrews 9:27).

Again, all religions are not teaching the same thing. Is man in an endless cycle of reincarnation or rebirth, or is his eternal destiny determined at death? Is there an immaterial essence that survives the death of the body, or are we material beings with no eternal soul or spirit?

Man's Solution

What is the answer to man's dilemma? Atheists teach that there is no immaterial soul that survives the death of the body. Therefore, man's duty is to propagate the human species. Hindus teach that man is trapped in an endless cycle of reincarnation. He can break this cycle by attaining enlightenment and discovering his true essence. Deliverance comes from changing one's beliefs about reality and one's identity. Buddhism teaches that man is trapped in an endless cycle of rebirth because of his desires for things of this world, which are an illusion. Man is not sinful; rather, he is ignorant regarding reality and his true nature. One must become enlightened to true reality by receiving the four noble truths, and then eliminate all desires by following the eightfold path.

Islam teaches that man is not sinful by nature but weak. Salvation comes by following the teachings of the *Quran*. Man must obey the teachings of Muhammad. On the day of judgment, his works will be weighed, and Allah will render his eternal destiny.

Christianity teaches that man is sinful and can do nothing to attain favor with God and eternal life. Salvation is accomplished by God's grace alone through the atoning work of Jesus. Salvation is a gift one is to receive; it cannot be earned by good works.

Look at the salvation message of the world religions and you will discover they are not teaching the same thing. In all the religions except Christianity, salvation is works-based. One must work to attain favor with Allah or enlightenment and freedom from the reincarnation or rebirth cycle. Christianity is based on grace, and one can do nothing to earn his or her salvation.

As is evident, the world's religions differ in fundamental ways. Steve Turner summed it up best stating, "We believe that all religions are basically the same. At least the one we read was. They all believe in love and goodness. They only differ on matters of creation, sin, heaven, hell, God and salvation." In other words, on the basic doctrines, the world religions present contradictory teachings. Since religions make mutually exclusive (contradictory) truth claims, pluralism cannot be true! The belief that all religions are true in the sense that they all bring us to God requires that we believe they are all false in what they objectively teach.

Logic argues against pluralism. Not only is pluralism logically incoherent, Jesus and the apostles rejected pluralism.

Jesus and the Apostles Rejected Pluralism

Few would argue that Jesus was the most loving and tolerant man who ever lived. Jesus reached out and ministered to those most despised by the culture. His sacrifice for all makes Him the most loving man who ever lived. However, when it came to truth about salvation, Jesus did not tolerate teachings that were false. On numerous occasions, He rebuked the religious leaders of His day, pointing out their error and hypocrisy.

On the teaching of salvation, Jesus stated, "I am the way, the truth, and the life. No one comes to the Father except through me" (John 14:6). Jesus claimed to be the embodiment of truth and the source of life. Since He is truth and life, eternal life is found in Him alone. Jesus did not claim to know a way but to literally be the *only* way to God.

In John 10:7–9, Jesus stated, "I tell you the truth, I am the gate for the sheep. All who ever came before me were thieves and robbers, but the sheep did not listen to them. I am the gate; whoever enters through me will be saved. He will come in and go out, and find pasture." Jesus made the exclusive claim to be the only true way to enter into the Father's kingdom.

In Matthew 7:13–14, Jesus stated, "Enter through the narrow gate. For wide is the gate and broad is the road that leads to destruction, and many enter through it. But small is the gate and narrow the road that leads to life, and only a few find it." Jesus emphasized that there is a narrow way to enter into eternal life, and there are many ways that are false and lead to destruction. Jesus taught that any way to salvation other than through Him was false.

The apostles repeated the teachings of Christ. In Acts 4:12, Peter stated, "Salvation is found in no one else, for there is no other name under heaven given to men by which we must be saved." Paul wrote in First Timothy 2:5, "For there is one God, and there is one mediator between God and men, the man Christ Jesus," Paul stated that there is only one who can intercede for man before a holy and righteous God, and that is Jesus Christ. All men are sinners. None can stand before a holy God. The nature of man keeps him from saving himself. Only the sinless, divine Son of God can bring us into the presence of a holy God.

Jesus confirmed His claim to be the divine Son of God through His miraculous, sinless life, death, and resurrection. Since Jesus is the divine Son of God, what He taught about salvation is true. Any teaching on salvation contrary to Christ's teaching must be false. Pluralism contradicts the teaching of Christ, and, therefore, it must be false.

What about Those Who Never Heard?

If Jesus is the only way to eternal life, what about those who have never heard the Gospel message? Is God just sending them to hell if they never had a chance to hear about Jesus? This poses one of the toughest questions for Christians. Hebrews 9:27 states that there is no second chance after death. The eternal fate of each person is determined by the decision they make during their life upon the earth. Has God revealed Himself to all people, so do they have a chance to respond to His invitation?

All people do indeed have an opportunity to respond to God. All people can respond to God through the witness of His creation and the conscience He has placed within each one of us. This is called general revelation. Romans 1:18–20 states:

> The wrath of God is being revealed from heaven against all the godlessness and wickedness of men who suppress the truth by their wickedness, since what may be known about God is plain to them,

because God has made it plain to them. For since the creation of the world God's invisible qualities—his eternal power and divine nature—have been clearly seen, being understood from what has been made, so that men are without excuse.

God has made Himself known to all men through His creation. Creation everyday is pointing to a creator. As discussed in Chapter 2, when a person studies the cosmos and life here upon the earth, one cannot ignore the design one sees throughout creation. Every design has a designer. In this way, creation points to an intelligent creator.

The second way God has made Himself known to all men is through the human conscience. Romans 2:15 teaches that the law of God is "written on the hearts" of all men. Our moral conscience not only helps us identify right and wrong, it also tells us that this moral law comes from a moral lawgiver, one to whom we will one day give an account of our lives. A universal moral law points to a moral lawgiver. Agnostic philosopher Immanuel Kant stated, "Two things fill the mind with ever new and increasing admiration and awe, the oftener and more steadily we reflect on them: the starry heavens above and the moral law within me"[6]

When individuals respond to general revelation, the witness of creation and the conscience, God is then responsible to bring the message of the Gospel or special revelation to them. For example, if a man living in the jungles of Africa looks up at the sky and acknowledges that there must be a creator who made all things, reflects upon his moral conscience, and concludes that there must be a moral lawgiver, he receives the witness of general revelation. If he then responds with a desire to know this creator, God is responsible to bring special revelation, the Gospel message, to him.

There are examples of this in the Bible. In Acts 8, an Ethiopian eunuch is a seeker of God. We know this because he was riding to Jerusalem to worship God and was reading the Old Testament book of Isaiah. Here was a man sincerely seeking to know God. God sends an angel to Philip who orders him to go to the road that goes from

---

[6] Immanuel Kant quoted in Norman Geisler, *Baker Encyclopedia of Christian Apologetics*. (Grand Rapids, MI.: Baker Books, 1999), 106.

Jerusalem to Gaza. There in the desert, Philip meets the eunuch, shares the Gospel with him, and the Ethiopian receives Christ.

Another example comes from Acts 10. This is the account of Cornelius, a God-fearing Roman captain. He obviously had acknowledged the witness of general revelation and was seeking to know God. God communicates to him in a dream to send men to summon Peter, who is in Joppa. At this time, God communicates to Peter in a vision that Roman soldiers are coming to escort him to the house of Cornelius. God brings the men together. Peter shares the Gospel with Cornelius, and he and his family receive Jesus.

We see in the Bible that when people receive the witness of general revelation, God brings special revelation to them. Not only do we see that in the Bible, we see examples of that even today. I interviewed a former Muslim from Bangladesh named Abraham Sarker. Abraham grew up in a Muslim country, and his father and grandfather were prominent Muslim leaders in the community. Abraham told me how he wanted to know God and would go to the Mosque regularly to pray and seek God. In his late teen years, he eagerly sought God. He prayed earnestly in the Mosque for God to make Himself known to him. Then, for a span of three nights, he had a nightmare that he stood before the judgment seat of Allah, and Allah threw him into hell. Abraham prayed zealously, asking Allah why he was having these dreams.

For the next few days, he prayed fervently, seeking an answer. He states that one morning at 4:30 a.m., he was anointed with some kind of mysterious oil. He did not know where it came from, but he felt reassured that Allah would answer him. Shortly after this incident, he was walking home and heard a voice say to him, "Go, and get a Bible." There were no Bibles available, but he remembered that voice. Four years later, he was sent to America as a Muslim missionary. The first thing he did was go to the public library, find a Bible, and read it. There he discovered the message of the Gospel and received Jesus Christ as His savior.[7]

There are numerous stories like Abraham Sarker's. When individuals acknowledge the witness of general revelation, God brings the Gospel

---

[7]   Abraham Sarker, *Understand My Muslim People* (Newberg, OR.: Barclay Press, 2004), 5-24.

message to them. Paul stated in Acts 14:15–17, "[God] who made heaven and earth and sea and everything in them. In the past, he let all nations go their own way. Yet he has not left himself without testimony: He has shown kindness by giving you rain from heaven and crops in their seasons; he provides you with plenty of food and fills your hearts with joy." God has made Himself known to all men through general revelation, and all men have an opportunity to know Him.

Conclusion

I was at the hospital to visit my uncle who had only a few days left to live. During my visit, my cousin asked to speak with me outside. My cousin Adrian remains one of my favorite cousins. During my high school years, he often took me out to play a round of golf with him. I greatly looked forward to those days and appreciated his thoughtfulness.

We stood outside in the hallway of the hospital, and he said to me, "Do you know why my father refused further dialysis treatment? It is because it was too much of a burden on all of us, so he has chosen to die rather than be a burden to all of us. Doesn't that make him a saint, Pat? Isn't that what religion is all about, sacrificing yourself for others?

I paused, prayed silently, and searched for the right words to say. How I wished I could have said, "Sure, there are many ways to God, and I am sure your father will be there in heaven." I longed to give words of comfort, but I knew I had to share a very difficult truth. I reluctantly said, "Your father is doing a very noble and courageous thing. However, eternal life depends on one thing: Do you know God's Son Jesus Christ? He is the only one who paid the price for our sin, and He is the only way to the Father." My cousin looked at me and said, "You know my parents are Buddhists, right?" I replied, "Yes, that is why I am concerned." With that, we returned to the hospital room, and I said my final good-bye to my uncle.

I do not take this teaching of Jesus lightly. I understand the implications of Jesus' words. Those who die without Christ will suffer eternal judgment and be separated from Christ for eternity. If pluralism were true, I would be its greatest champion. But sometimes the teachings of Christ and truth can be difficult and painful to hear. However, we cannot reject this teaching just because it is hard. To preach a gospel of pluralism is to preach a false gospel.

It is for this reason that the apostles gave their lives to bring the Gospel to the far reaches of the Roman Empire. The love for others continues to drive many Christians today to go throughout the world and preach the good news of Jesus Christ. Since Jesus is the only way to God, every believer in Christ must take part in fulfilling the Great Commission, to make disciples of Christ throughout the world.

CONCLUSION

Realize the Hope

Thomas entered the doorway cautiously. He thought to himself, *I will not give way to their emotion. I love these men, and we have been through a lot together, but I will not be convinced by their words. Unless I see, I will not believe.*

With this determination, he entered and was embraced by the men. "Thomas, we have seen Jesus!" they exclaimed. He was here among us! We touched Him, and He showed us His hands and His side!" The excitement in that room was moving. A new sense of peace and joy had transformed these men. Thomas sensed something had happened, but life transformation was not the proof he was looking for.

Nathaniel, the once sarcastic one, was the first to invite Thomas to sit at the table and hear his story. The other men followed; as each one shared what they had witnessed, Thomas listened intently. He asked them detailed questions to find any inconsistency in their accounts. At the final question, the men waited for Thomas' response. He was fighting the emotions that wrestled in his heart. His friends were convincing in their accounts, but if he was going to surrender his life again to this Jesus, he needed to see a risen savior. *Unless I see, I cannot believe*, he thought to himself. As he gazed at his cup, the others waited to hear what their friend had to say.

Suddenly, they all gasped with exultation as Jesus appeared in their midst. It was specifically for Thomas that He appeared at this time.

Thomas' eyes widened and his mouth dropped as he stared at Jesus. The fire of joy, excitement, and surprise raced through every cell of his body. This was not an illusion. This was real!

With love in his eyes, Jesus held out his hands to Thomas and gently said, "Put your finger here; see my hands. Reach out your hand, and put it into my side. Stop doubting and believe."

Thomas slowly moved across the room and made his way to Jesus. He put his right hand on the nail mark in Jesus' left wrist first and then on his right. The wounds were healed, but the inch-and-a half-wide scars were still there. He then examined the pierced side of Jesus and saw the scar left by the Roman spear. It was about two and a half inches wide, but fully healed.

With eyes the size of saucers, Thomas gazed into the eyes of God the Son and exclaimed, "My Lord and my God!" It was true. Jesus had risen, and He was alive. As Thomas clung to Jesus' left hand, Jesus embraced him. Overwhelmed with joy, tears began to flow down Thomas' face. The other ten gathered around the two, filled with joy at seeing their friend acknowledging the joyous truth they had come to know. Then Jesus looked into the eyes of Thomas and said, "Because you have seen Me, you have believed; blessed are those who have not seen and yet have believed."

A small stack of books rested next to my floor cushion. I had read each book to examine the evidence for the Christian faith. I tested these facts by questioning professors and teachers who were skeptics. Many confident critics were unable to refute the evidence I presented, and now the tables had turned. On a sunny, May morning, I finished the final chapter of my last book and laid the book down. I sat quietly reflecting on what I had learned and quietly whispered, "It's true. All of this is true." My search had come to an end. Jesus said, "You will know the truth, and the truth shall set you free." I surrendered my life to Him, and I was free.

The evidence lay before me; this was not a mirage in the desert. The Bible was God's Word, Jesus was God incarnate, and He had risen from the dead. I knew I would never look at life in the same way. Jesus stood before me with His arms stretched open and said, "Come. Put your finger here and feel the nail prints in my hands." I had come to learn that there was enough reason and evidence to believe.

You Can Know God Personally

A dynamic relationship with God can be a reality in your life by believing the good news. This is the Gospel message:

God loves you and desires to have a personal relationship with you. However, we cannot experience this love relationship because we have disobeyed God and chosen to live the way we desire with no regard for Him. This attitude is called sin, and this separates us from God.

Although God is loving, He is just, and the price of sin is eternal separation from God, or eternal death in hell. In His love, God sent Jesus, God the Son, to die in our place and pay the penalty of sin. Justice has been fulfilled on the cross; the price of sin has been paid.

All that is required of you is to:

1. Confess or agree with God that you have sinned and express your sorrow for rejecting Him.
2. Accept His offer of forgiveness by placing your trust in Jesus, who died for your sins and rose again, conquering sin and death.
3. Personally receive Jesus as your only Savior and Lord of your life.

If this is the desire of your heart, then pray this prayer. It is not just the words that bring you into relationship with God, but the sincerity of your heart.

"Dear Jesus. I agree that I have sinned by choosing to live my way and rejecting You. I ask for forgiveness for my disobedience. Thank you for sending Jesus to pay the price of my sin. I believe that He died in my place and rose again, conquering sin and death. Today I receive you as the Savior and Lord of my life. In Jesus' name. Amen."

If this is the sincere desire of your heart, you have become a new creation. Everything has now changed. Paul states in Second Corinthians 5:17, "Therefore, if anyone is in Christ, he is a new creation. The old has gone; the new has come!"

You now have a personal relationship with God. John 1:12 states, "Yet to all who received Him, to those who believed in His name, He gave the right to become children of God." You have received the assurance of eternal life with God. John 5:24 states, "I tell you the truth, whoever hears My word and believes Him who sent Me has eternal life and will not be condemned; he has crossed over from death to life." The empowering presence of Christ will always remain with you, for He has indwelt you with His Holy Spirit to abide in your heart forever. Jesus states in John 14:15–17, "If you love Me, you will obey what I command. And I will ask the Father, and He will give you another Counselor to be with you forever—the Spirit of Truth."

There are many more promises to be experienced in the new life of a believer. There is the promise of everlasting joy, everlasting peace, fullness of life, and much more. These can be found in God's Word, the Bible. It is my suggestion that you begin your new life in Christ with a daily Scripture reading, beginning in the book of John. Knowing God does not mean one will have an easy and pain-free life. Trials and tribulations will come, but Jesus gives us the hope and the ability to overcome the difficulties that we will face through the power of the risen Christ.

The hope of every man, woman, and child is found in a person, the person of Jesus Christ. In my personal quest, Jesus revealed His nail-pierced hands and wounded side to me. It is my sincere hope that He has done the same for you. This book is not an exhaustive work on the evidence for the Christian faith. This book was designed to confirm a Christian's beliefs and to challenge unbelievers to consider the faith. For some, I am sure it answered their questions. For others, I hope it piqued some interest to begin your own search for the truth.

Tradition teaches that Thomas became one of the greatest evangelists of the twelve disciples of Jesus. He ventured all the way to India to preach the message of the risen Jesus, of whom he had once refused to believe. There in India he died as a martyr. He was tied to a stake and run through with a lance. A church still exists there dedicated to this wonderful disciple whose honesty has led us to hear some of the greatest words ever taught by Jesus. Thomas' words, "Unless I see … " have been shared by all those who search for the truth in the same manner. I hope that for some of you your faith is renewed. I hope for others you can say, "I now see, and I believe."

BIBLIOGRAPHY

Alberge, Dalya. "Museum's Tablet Lends New Weight to Biblical Truth." *The Times* 11 July 2007, http://www.timesonline.co.uk/tol/comment/faith/article2056362.ece.

Albright, William F. *Archaeology and the Religion of Israel.* Baltimore: John Hopkins, 1953.

Anderson, Norman. *Christianity and the World Religions.* Downer's Grove, IL: InterVarsity, 1984.

Archer, Gleason. *A Survey of Old Testament Introduction.* Chicago Moody Press, 1985.

Barna, George. *Third Millenium Teens.* Ventura, CA: Barna Research Group, 1999.

Beckwith, Francis, and Greg Koukl, *Relativism: Feet Planted in Mid Air.* Grand Rapids, MI: Baker Books, 1998.

Boa, Kenneth. *I am Glad You Asked.* Colorado Springs:Victor Books, 1994.

Bohlin, Ray. *Creation, Evolution, and Modern Science.* Grand Rapids, MI: Kregel Publications, 2000.

Brown, Collin ed. *Dictionary of New Testament Theology.* Grand Rapids: Zondervan Publishing, 1986.

Brown, Dan. *The Da Vinci Code*. New York: Doubleday 2003.

Brown, Francis, Driver, S.R. and Briggs, Charles. *The Brown-Driver-Briggs Hebrew and English Lexicon*. Peabody, MA.: Hendrickson Publishers, 1979.

Bruce, F. F. *The New Testament Documents: Are They Reliable?* Downers Grove, IL: InterVarsity Press, 1983.

Bukkyo Dendo Kyokai. *The Teaching of the Buddha*. Tokyo: Kosaido Printing Company, 1996.

Carson, Donald. *The Gagging of God: Christianity Confronts Pluralism*. Grand Rapids, MI: 1996.

Collins, Francis. *The Language of God*. New York: Free Press, 2006.

Colson, Charles. *How Now Shall We Live?* Wheaton, IL: Tyndale House Publishers, 1999.

Copan, Paul. *That's Just Your Interpretation*. Grand Rapids, MI: Baker Books, 2001.

Craig, William Lane. *Reasonable Faith: Christian Truth and Apologetics*. Wheaton: Crossway, 1994.

_____. *The Son Rises: Historical Evidence for the Resurrection of Jesus*. Chicago: Moody Press, 1981.

Crossan, John Dominic. *Jesus: A Revolutionary Biography*. San Francisco, CA: Harper Collins Publishers, 1989.

Darwin, Charles. *The Origin of Species*. New York: Collier Books, 1962.

Dawkins, Richard. *The God Delusion*. New York, New York: Houghton Mifflin Company, 2006. Evans, Craig *Fabricating Jesus*. Downers Grove, IL: InterVarsity Press, 2006.

Flew, Antony. *There is no a God: How the World's Most Notorious Atheist Changed His Mind*. New York: Harper One, 2007.

Freke, Timothy and Gandy, Peter. *The Laughing Jesus*. New York: Three Rivers Press, 2005.

Gaebelein, Frank, ed. *The Expositor's Bible Commentary*. Grand Rapids: Zondervan, 1986.

Garstang, John. *The Foundations of Bible History: Joshua, Judges*. London: Constable, 1931.

Geisler, Norman and Brooks, Ron. *When Skeptics Ask*. Wheaton, IL: Victor Press, 1990.

_____. *Baker Encyclopedia of Christian Apologetics*. Grand Rapids, MI: Baker Books, 1999.

Geisler, Norman, and T.A. Howe. *When Critics Ask: A Popular Handbook on Bible Difficulties*. Wheaton, IL: Victor Books, 1992.

Geisler, Norman, and William Nix. *A General Introduction to the Bible*. Chicago: Moody Press, 1986.

Geisler, Norman, and Abdul Saleeb. *Answering Islam*. Grand Rapids, MI: Baker Books, 2002.

Geisler, Norman, and Frank Turek. *I Don't Have Enough Faith to be an Atheist*. Wheaton, IL: Crossway Books, 2004.

Geivett, Douglas, and Gary Habermas. *In Defense of Miracles*. Downers Grove, IL: InterVarsity Press, 1997.

Glueck, Nelson. *Rivers in the Desert: A History of the Negev*. New York: Farrar, Strauss, and Cudahy, 1959.

Glynn, Patrick. *God the Evidence*. Rocklin, CA: Prima Publishing, 1997.

Greenleaf, Simon. *The Testimony of the Evangelists: The Gospels Examined by the Rules of Evidence*. Grand Rapids, MI: Kregal Publications, 1995.

Groothuis, Douglas. *Truth Decay*. Downers Grove, IL: 2000.

Habermas, Gary. *The Historical Jesus*. Joplin, MO: College Press Publishing, 1997.

Hemer, Colin. *The Book of Acts in the Setting of Hellenistic History*. Winona Lake, IN: Eisenbrauns, 2001.

Hoerth, Alfred. *Archaeology and the Old Testament*. Grand Rapids, MI: Baker Book House, 1998.

Hume, David. *An Enquiry Concerning Human Understanding*. Oxford, England: Clarendon Press, 1957.

Ishaq, Ibn. *The Life of Muhammad,* trans. A. Guillaume. Karachi, Pakistan: Oxford University Press, 1955.

Jastrow, Robert. *God and the Astronomers*. New York: Norton & Company, 1992.

Johnson, Philip. *Darwin on Trial*. Downers Grove, IL: InterVarsity Press, 1991.

Jones, Timothy. *Conspiracies and the Cross*. Lake Mary, FL: Strang Publications, 2008.

Josephus, Flavius. *The Works of Josephus*. Translated by William Whiston. Peabody, MA: Hendrickson Publishing, 1987.

Kenyon, Kathleen and Holland, Thomas. *Excavations at Jericho Vol. 3: The Architecture and Stratigraphy of the Tell*. London: BSA.

Komoszewski, Ed, James Sawyer, and Daniel Wallace, *Reinventing Jesus*. Grand Rapids, MI: Kregel Publications, 2006.

Kreeft, Peter and Ronald Tacelli. *Handbook of Christian Apologetics*. Downers Grove, IL: InterVarsity Press, 1994.

LaHaye, Tim. *Jesus: Who Is He?* Sisters, OR: Multnomah Books, 1996.

Lewis, C. S. *Mere Christianity*. New York: Macmillan Publishing, 1960.

_____. *Miracles*. New York: Macmillan Publishing, 1960.

Licona, Michael. *The Resurrection of Jesus*. Downers Grove, IL: InterVarsity Press, 2010.

Little, Paul. *Know Why You Believe*. Downers Grove, IL: InterVarsity Press, 1988.

McCallum, Dennis ed. *The Death of Truth*. Minneapolis: Bethany House Publishers, 1996.

McDowell, Josh. *The New Evidence That Demands a Verdict*. San Bernardino, CA: Here's Life Publishers, 1979.

_____. McDowell, Josh. *The Last Christian Generation*. Holiday, FL: Green Key Books, 2006.

_____. *The Resurrection Factor*. San Bernardino, CA: Here's Life Publishers, 1981.

McDowell, Josh and Bob Hostetler. *The New Tolerance*. Wheaton, IL: Tyndale House Publishers, 1998.

McGrath, Alister. *Intellectuals Don't Need God and Other Modern Myths*. Grand Rapids: Zondervan, 1993.

McNeil, William. *A World History*. New York: Oxford University Press, 1979.

McRay, John. *Archaeology and the New Testament*. Grand Rapids, MI: Baker Book House, 1991.

Montgomery, John, ed. *Evidence for Faith*. Dallas: Probe Books, 1991.

Moreland, J. P. *Scaling the Secular City*. Grand Rapids, MI: Baker Book House, 1987.

Morison, Frank. *Who Moved the Stone?* Grand Rapids, MI: Zondervan Publishing, 1958.

Nash, Ronald. *Faith and Reason*. Grand Rapids, MI: Zondervan Publishing, 1988.

_____. *Gospel and the Greeks*. Dallas: Word Books, 1992.

_____. *Is Jesus the Only Savior?* Grand Rapids, MI: Zondervan, 1994.

_____. *Worldviews in Conflict: Choosing Christianity in a World of Ideas*. Grand Rapids: Zondervan, 1992.

Netland, Harold. *Encountering Religious Pluralism*. Downers Grove, IL: InterVarsity Press, 2001.

Nietzche, Friedrich, "The Gay Science," in *The Portable Nietzsche*, Walter Kaufman ed. New York: Viking, 1954.

Payne, J. Barton. *Encyclopedia of Biblical Prophecy.* New York: Harper and Row, 1973.

Pentecost, Dwight. *The Words and Works of Christ.* Grand Rapids: Zondervan Publishing, 1981.

Prabhupada, Bhaktivedanta. *Beyond Birth and Death.* Australia: The Bhaktivedanta Book Trust, 1999.

Price, Randall. *The Stones Cry Out.* Eugene, OR: Harvest House Publishers, 1997.

Rana, Fazale, and Hugh Ross. *Origins of Life.* Colorado Springs, CO: NavPress, 2004.

Renard, John. *Responses Top 101 Questions on Buddhism.* New York: Paulist Press, 1999.

Reynolds, Nigel. "Tiny Tablet Provides Proof for Old Testament," *Telegraph.co.uk.* 13 July 2007, http://www.telegraph.co.uk/news/main.jhtm l;jsessionid=OE1Y2OKKNRS3PQFIQMFSF FWAVCBQ0IV0?xml=/news/2007/07/11/ntablet111.xml.

Richard, Ramesh. *The Population of Heaven.* Chicago: Moody Press, 1994.

Ross, Hugh. *The Creator and the Cosmos.* Colorado Springs: NavPress Publishing, 1995

Russell, Bertrand. *Why I Am Not a Christian.* New York: Simon & Schuster, 1957.

Sarker, Abraham. *Understand My Muslim People.* Newberg, OR: Barclay Press, 2004.

Schafer, Peter. *Jesus in the Talmud.* Princeton, NJ.: Princeton University Press, 2007.

Schumacher, Stephen, and Gert Woerner, ed. *The Encyclopedia of Eastern Philosophy and Religion.* Boston: Shambhala Publications, 1994.

Simpson, George. *The Meaning of Evolution.* New Haven, CT: Yale University Press, 1967.

Sire, James. *The Universe Next Door: A Basic Worldview Catalog*, 3rd ed. Downers Grove, InterVarsity Press, 1997.

Stott, John. *Basic Christianity*. Downers Grove, IL: Inter Varsity Press, 1971.

Strauss, David. *The Life of Jesus for the People*, Vol. 1, 2nd edition. London: Williams and Norgate, 1879.

Strobel, Lee. *The Case for Christ*. Grand Rapids: Zondervan, 2000.

_____. *The Case for a Creator*. Grand Rapids, MI: Zondervan Publishing, 2004.

_____. *The Case for Faith*. Grand Rapids, MI: Zondervan Publishing, 2000.

_____. *The Case for the Real Jesus*. Grand Rapids, MI: Zondervan Publishing, 2007.

Tsang, Reginald. "Congratulations, Your Baby Has a Mutation?" *Science and Faith*, Volume 1 Issue 2, December 2006.

Vanderkam, James, and Peter Flint. *The Meaning of the Dead Sea Scrolls*. San Francisco, CA: Harper Collins Publishers, 2002.

Veith, Gene Edward. *Postmodern Times*. Wheaton, IL: Crossway Books, 1994.

Walvoord, John. *Prophecy Knowledge Handbook*. Wheaton, IL: Victor Press, 1990.

_____. *Daniel: The Key to Prophetic Revelation*. Chicago: Moody Press, 1971.

Jeffrey Weiss, "Study: Most Americans Say Many Religions Can Lead to Eternal Life," *Dallas Morning News*, (24 June 2008).

Wells, Jonathan. *Icons of Evolution*. Washington DC: Regenery Publishing, 2000.

White, A.N. Sherwin. *Roman Society and Roman Law in the New Testament*. Oxford: Clarendon, 1963.

Wilford, John. "Archaeologists say Evidence of House of David Found." *Dallas Morning News,* (6 August 1993): 1A.

Witmer, John. *Immanuel.* Nashville: Word Publishing, 1998.

Wood, Bryant. "Did the Israelites Conquer Jericho? A New Look at the Archaeological Evidence," *Biblical Archaeological Review,* Vol. XVI, No. 2, (March/April 1990): 44–58.

Wright, Fred. *Highlights of Archaeology in the Bible Lands.* Chicago: Moody Press, 1955.

Yamauchi, Edwin. *The Stones and the Scriptures.* Philadelphia: J. B. Lippen Lott Company, 1972.

Zacharias, Ravi. *Jesus Among Other Gods.* Nashville: Word Publishing, 2000.

ABOUT THE AUTHOR

Patrick Zukeran received graduate degrees from Dallas Theological Seminary (ThM) and Southern Evangelical Seminary (D.Min). He is the Executive Director of Evidence and Answers a Christian research and teaching ministry specializing in Christian apologetics. He hosts a national and international radio show, Evidence and Answers. He has a national and international speaking and teaching ministry. He has authored several books including, *The Apologetics of Jesus,* co-authored with Norman Geisler and *God, Eternity, and Spirituality.*

Contact Information

To order additional copies of this book, please visit
www.redemption-press.com.
Also available on Amazon.com and BarnesandNoble.com
Or by calling toll free 1-844-2REDEEM.